PUBLISHED ON THE MARY CADY TEW MEMORIAL FUND.

The Corridors of Time · IX ·

THE LAW AND THE PROPHETS

By HAROLD PEAKE and
HERBERT JOHN FLEURE

NEW HAVEN · YALE UNIVERSITY PRESS
LONDON · HUMPHREY MILFORD
OXFORD UNIVERSITY PRESS
1936

Printed in England at the OXFORD UNIVERSITY PRESS
by John Johnson, Printer to the University

PREFACE

THE concluding volume of our chronological series, figuratively speaking, ends our walk down the corridors of time from the dawn of human life to the periods when written ideas and abstract thought spread far and wide. We have tried to weave into a connected story the facts observed by specialists, not hesitating to advance, in a tentative spirit, hypotheses that may be modified by further study. It seems to us that Gräbner's doctrines of the diffusion of culture, and the theories of parallel evolution of culture in different lands, are both of value, and that not infrequently both sets of factors are found acting together. Indeed, we think that culture contacts, except when involving complete destruction on one side or the other, have not only provided mutual enrichment by exchange, but have also stimulated fresh developments. Since such contacts have enabled some of the more active minds in the affected zone to rise out of their traditional prejudices, they have raised such minds to a level of objectivity that promotes freedom of thought. This has been a great stimulus to social and cultural development and a most essential tonic for the maintenance of social health.

Later periods, with more abundant written records, have been reviewed in many works and require different treatment, since, in dealing with them, the scholar has far greater trouble with questions of prejudicial statement. He is able to give more detailed accounts; it is not so certain that he can as adequately grasp the broader truths. In a volume which will be supplementary rather than strictly a continuation of this series, we shall attempt to review the processes of racial and social evolution of man in general terms.

Many thanks are due to the authors, editors, and publishers of the following works and journals for permission to reproduce figures: *Reallexikon der Vorgeschichte*, vol. xiii (Walter de Gruyter & Co., Berlin) for fig. 4 *c*; *Ancient Egypt*, by G. Rawlinson (T. Fisher Unwin Ltd. (Ernest Benn Ltd.)) for figs. 6 and 10; *Assyria*, by Z. A. Ragozin (T. Fisher Unwin Ltd. (Ernest Benn Ltd.)) for figs. 7–9, 12, and 18; *Studien zur Kunst des Ostens*, by J. Strzygowski (Avalun-Verlag, Hellerau) for fig. 25; *Census of India*, 1931, vol. i (India), pt. i (Report), by J. H. Hutton (Office of the High Commissioner for India) for figs. 26–9; *Mohenjo-Daro and the Indus Civilization*, edited by Sir John Marshall (Arthur Probsthain) for fig. 30; *Buddhastatuen*, by L. Adam (Verlag Strecker und Schröder, Stuttgart) for fig. 31; *La civilisation primitive en Italie*, by O. Montelius (The Swedish Academy) for fig. 35; *The Cemeteries of Etruria*, vol. ii, by G. Dennis (John Murray) for fig. 37; *A Guide to Antiquities of the Early Iron Age* (British Museum) for figs. 40 and 50; *Manuel d'archéologie préhistorique celtique et gallo-romaine*, vol. ii, pt. ii, by J. Déchelette (Librairie A. Picard, Paris) for fig. 45; *The Early Iron Age Inhabited Site at All Cannings Cross Farm, Wiltshire*, by M. E. Cunnington (George Simpson & Co., Devizes, Ltd.) for fig. 46; *The Victoria History of the County of Berkshire*, vol. i, for fig. 49; *The Glastonbury Lake Village*, vol. i, by A. Bulleid and H. St. G. Gray (Glastonbury Antiquarian Society) for fig. 51 *a* and *b*; *Greek Coins*, by J. G. Milne (Clarendon Press) for fig. 15; *Iranians and Greeks in South Russia*, by M. Rostovtzeff (Clarendon Press) for fig. 2; *The Iron Age in Italy*, by D. Randall-MacIver (Clarendon Press) for fig. 34; and *Villanovans and Early Etruscans*, by D. Randall-MacIver (Clarendon Press) for fig. 36.

May 1936

H. J. E. P.
H. J. F.

CONTENTS

LIST OF ILLUSTRATIONS

I

The Revival of the Northern Steppe

IN volume v of this series, *The Steppe and the Sown*, in agreement
with Rostovtzeff, Ebert, and Childe, we ascribed some elaborate
tombs in the Kuban to the third millennium B.C., though Tallgren dates them in the second. They indicate a civilization
using stone and copper, and having characteristic battle-axes
derived, as we think with Childe, from Mesopotamian models of
earlier times. Some were in copper and others in stone; the
latter were, we think, derivatives of those in metal, and spread
into north-west Europe, where they played a very important
part in the early civilization of the west Baltic area. This civilization may have continued in the steppe into the second millennium B.C., but so far as our limited knowledge goes there was
little activity in the grasslands of south Russia in the second half
of that period, which, we have reason to think from observations
made in the Baltic region and in Switzerland, was one of warm
and dry summers. The Crimea, the Kuban, and the Taman
peninsula, with more maritime climates, probably retained
larger populations. We think that the movement of steppe
peoples outwards in the third, and the first half of the second,
millennium B.C. was connected with the spread of the Aryan
languages already mentioned in our volume iii, *Peasants and
Potters*, and volume vii, *Merchant Venturers in Bronze*.

The modern connexions between south Russia and lands
farther west, in central Europe, are chiefly along the loess belt
north of the Carpathian arc, or up parts of the Danube, but
there is an important hint of another connexion in the survival
of Ruthenian speech in the extreme east of Czechoslovakia, the
area called Carpathian Ruthenia within the mountain arc. It is
important to remember that while the way along the loess by
Lwow and probably Cracow has been important from time

immemorial, that along the Danube had severe limitations until the rise of modern engineering. The difficulty was the Kazan defile with the Iron Gates at its lower extremity. The river itself was here too difficult until power-driven boats were available, and it required Roman engineering skill, under Trajan, to make a temporary way along the precipitous gorge by building

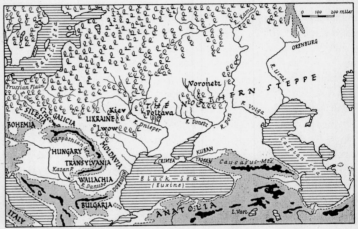

FIG. 1. Map of the Northern Steppe and its surroundings.

out a widening of a rock ledge by means of a wooden platform on oblique supports driven into holes made in the rock beneath. Detours avoiding the defile do exist but are themselves difficult, and it seems that early cultures of Moldavia and Wallachia did not to any extent spread westwards through the defile or the detours that just avoid it.

On the other hand, the difficulties that the gradients of the Carpathian arc present to modern railways were not without compensations in early times. These mountains and the Transylvanian Alps are not a close-set sequence of rocky peaks covered with perpetual snow such as one finds in the Swiss Alps. The Carpathian system after its uplift, in what geologists call the Mesozoic Era, was planed down, and then re-uplifted as a block in the Miocene period to be dissected afresh. The result is that on the Carpathian heights there are great stretches of grassland above the forested slopes of the sharply-cut river valleys, which have made a complex drainage pattern that gives several passes between east and west. These communications seem to have had considerable importance in former times.

Parvan, in his book *Dacia*, gives a valuable picture of a considerable development of civilization during the last part of the second millennium B.C. in Transylvania, which we know was famous for gold and other metals as well as for salt. This civilization, Parvan says, was related to that of Bohemia and western Hungary, and profited by connexions with Italy, while its links with the lands around the Black Sea were slight, and it was free from invasion from the east. This supports the view put forward above that the steppe of south Russia was inactive at the time.

Tallgren shows that this Transylvanian culture spread to Moldavia and as far as the Dnieper below Kiev, as may be inferred from hoards containing sickles, bronze battle-axes, rings and penannular objects, socketed lance-heads and axes, which last suggest a date that may be well after 1000 B.C. The culture had a further extension to the Donetz, Don, and lower Kama, but hoards in the Caucasus, which seem to be more or less contemporary, are without the socketed axe. This suggests that the culture, spreading from Transylvania into the steppes in the early part of the last millennium B.C., did not cross the steppe south-eastwards.

Ebert emphasizes the importance of Iranian place-names west of the Don and their absence east of this river, as well as their rarity in the Taman peninsula and the Kuban, which were probably inhabited by an old population known to Herodotus as the Sauromatians.

The spread into the steppe is, in our opinion, a result of cooler and moister summers at that time, and we have evidence of such a change, at any rate from Denmark and Switzerland, and from parts of the Mediterranean region. The lack of a spread of culture from Transylvania and Moldavia across the steppe to the Caucasus is understood when we realize that the steppe was becoming occupied by horsed warriors. The Cimmerians, whose kings had Aryan names, and were related, according to Ebert, to Iranians or, according to Rostovtzeff, to Thracians, were an early group of such conquerors. As they attacked the kingdom of Van in Armenia in the eighth century and Assyria in the seventh, they were evidently disturbed; ancient writers state that the Scythians were the conquerors at this date.

The Scythians, arising as a power probably in the Don basin, seem to have separated the older peoples into a Ukrainian-Thracian-Transylvanian group on the west, and a Cimmerian, with older elements, on the south-east.

Some remarkable graves of the Kuban basin have been the subject of much discussion in this connexion. Some of the best were found at Elizavetinskaia Stanica. A long passageway, 25 by $3\frac{1}{2}$ metres, had been made with a large mound at its end, and it contained two wagons with iron-rimmed twelve-spoked wheels, drawn by six horses; it was roofed with timber. The mound itself enclosed a chamber which was a square, with sides measuring 8·85 metres, covered with timber and itself including a stone cist in the north-east corner. Outside the chamber, in the re-entrant angles between the chamber and the passage, was found on the west a row of nine horse skeletons, and on the east four skeletons of men with bead necklaces. On the north side of the chamber was a man's grave with remains of a wagon and horses, but whether of the period of the main grave or not is uncertain. Ornaments in beaten gold included a medusa head design, palmettes, and lotus flowers. In another mound were buried with

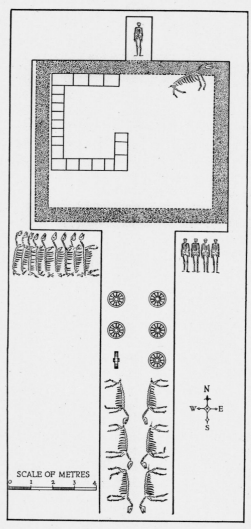

SCALE OF METRES

0   1   2   3   4

FIG. 2. Barrow at Elizavetinskaia.

the prince seven women, and the stone cist in this case was in the centre of the chamber; the breastpiece of a suit of armour found in this was decorated with a medusa head. Ebert thinks some of these graves may be pre-Scythian or very early Scythian. The analogies with the Mesopotamian graves of the fourth millennium B.C. discovered by Woolley at Ur are most striking.

There, in deep chambers with corbelled or domed roofs, were found the burials of kings accompanied by their women and their treasure, their servants, sentries, oxen, and two wagons. In one case, sixty bodies, including six armed sentries and six oxen, give a suggestion of the importance of the number six in the ritual of Ur, and the same number is emphasized in the Kuban graves. There may be two and a half millennia or more between their dates, and this makes the resemblance the more impressive. Childe has argued that, if these graves of the Kuban are Scythian, we must not call the Scythians Iranian, as these grave-rites belong to an immensely older period. Ebert says that it would be better to use the graves as an argument for the non-Iranian character of the people of the Kuban district in pre-Scythian and early Scythian times. There may have been a survival here of the mode of life of the third millennium B.C., at which time the Kuban was in touch with Mesopotamia or with elements of a culture akin to that of the land between the rivers.

The hypothesis we adopt is that, in the Kuban at least, there have been survivals from a remote past giving some continuity during the millennia of pre-Roman history, and that the neighbouring steppe has been from time to time ruled by successive groups of horsed warriors, who have intermingled with the older inhabitants and been ultimately submerged under later conquests. One of these groups of horsed warriors would be the Cimmerians with Iranian relationships and with power over the equally Aryan-speaking but more definitely European-Aryan inhabitants of the Ukraine. Perhaps this is illustrative less of the widespread tendency of the nomad to dominate the peasant and more of the domination by the mobile horseman of the less mobile wheeled nomads equipped with ox-carts.

The undoubted Scythian graves show the large sacrifices of

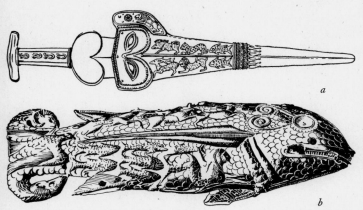

FIG. 3. Gold objects of Scythic workmanship from Vettersfelde.

women, sentries, servants, and animals, and there is often a wooden construction, in tent form or in the form of a wooden house, above the actual burial, the whole being covered by a great mound. These graves occur in the Kuban, the Taman peninsula, and the Crimea, as well as in the region of Kiev and the lower Dnieper, in Poltava, in Voronetz and the Don basin, and in the Volga and Ural areas; Scythic finds farther west indicate the spreading of the Scythians north of the Carpathian mountain ring into east Galicia, Silesia, and the Prussian plain, along one of the great loess belts. The point farthest west that has yielded a definitely Scythic collection of objects is Vettersfelde, about six miles south-south-east of Guben, a town at the junction of the Lubis and the Neisse, a left bank tributary of the Oder. This find, which belongs to the late sixth century B.C., is specially rich in gold, and includes a much-decorated golden fish, ear-rings and pendants, chains and neck-rings, and a short iron sword with golden scabbard; this shows archaic Greek influences in its decoration.

The Scythians spread through the Carpathian passes into Hungary and south-westwards into Wallachian Rumania and Bulgaria, attaining their maximum importance in the west about the sixth century B.C. The Iron Gates and the Kazan defile proved themselves an effective barrier to these peoples. That the Scythians included a princely element akin to the Iranians seems certain, but, along with this, there were elements from the older populations of south Russia, as well as of so-called Mongolian peoples. The centre of the Scythian power, which lasted from the late seventh to the fourth century B.C., was the region between the Dnieper and the Don. The Scythians were contemporary with the Greek colonists on the Euxine coasts and the Dnieper.

A good deal is known about Scythic equipment and art. Their typical sword was a short two-edged weapon with gold plating on the hilt or pommel. They used a short bow and short feathered arrows with tips usually of bronze but sometimes of iron or bone or even of stone. Lances and throwing-spears were common; battle-axes appear to have survived in the Kuban area but not on the lower Dnieper. The insignia of important personages include small bronze axes as well as stone and copper club-heads, survivals from older phases of culture. Iron knives were made with bone handles. Shields were long and rectangular with the corners rounded off. Armour was worn in the form of scale-coats on a leather or wool basis and the scales might be of bone, bronze, or iron.

The men wore long trousers and coats with fur trimmings, as

well as helmets and diadems. Safety-pins appear only late in the
Scythian period. The women wore pleated skirts and a mantle-
like over-garment; sometimes they had veils. Rings and brace-

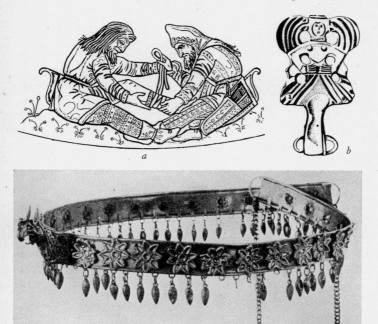

a

b

c

FIG. 4. Scythian attire.

lets were widely used, and mirrors, showing Greek influence,
were common.

Metal pieces of horse equipment were very important, and,
late in the period, became most elaborate. The whip was in

general use, but not the spur. Wagons were obviously of great importance.

Apparently they often lived in tents and wooden constructions modified from the idea of the tent, but near the Black Sea coasts their dwellings were considerably influenced by the proximity of the Greek settlers.

The use of animal forms in ornaments was a great feature of their art, and representations of the deer abound, as well as many of the hare, especially in the more purely steppe areas. The horse's form was less used for this purpose. Lions and goats, birds' heads and fishes are often represented, and there is a good deal of Greek influence observable in detail. The question of the origins and factors of development of the animal style in Scythic ornament is much discussed. Some believe it to be of eastern origin and to have relations with the Iranian culture. Ebert seems rather of the opinion that a good deal of it is a local development in the west of the steppe under Greek and other influences interacting one on another. Of eastern elements, with Iranian relationships, one may mention, following Rostovtzeff, the animals with their fore-parts spreading in one direction and their hind-parts in another, the animals on pole-tops, and the animals distorted to fit them into a particular space, especially with the head reversed. The use of animal figures for decorative purposes, and the posture given to the animal's head on the base of the sword-hilt figured, are very characteristic.

The Scythic style has by some been supposed to be derived from that seen in Bronze Age art in Minussinsk, western Siberia, but Rostovtzeff thinks Turkestan a more likely home from which Iran and south Russia on the one hand, and China on the other, received this influence. Borovka seeks the origin in the Stone Age art of the north, which has seemed to some critics a source too remote in place and time; in time, however, it need not be remote at all. Hornblower, who published in *Man*, May 1933,

FIG. 5. Types of Scythic art.

a study of the dragons or mythical animals in early Asiatic art, thinks that Mesopotamian influence, combined with Stone Age northern Asiatic art, gave birth to the Scythic style, which, as time went on, was more and more influenced by the Greek. Scythian ideas exerted a strong influence on China, with the introduction of the horse for riding and new details of military equipment in the third century B.C., when first the T'sin and then the Han dynasty replaced the Chou.

At this period of change the west of the steppe was stirring too. From at least the middle of that century the ruling people in south Russia were the Sarmatians, who seem to have absorbed the Scythians, save such as took refuge in the Crimea and the Dobrudja. Former statements about fundamental contrasts between Scythian and Sarmatian graves are to be discounted, but the goods of the latter are on the whole poorer, and silver to some extent replaces gold. It is thought that Sarmatian graves are older in Orenburg, where they go back to the early fifth century, than they are farther west. The battle-axe is rare among Sarmatians, but the helmet is commoner than in earlier periods, and so is the *fibula*, which shows central European forms assigned to the La Tène period. The animal style in decoration, which had been declining, was revived under the Sarmatians, a point which adds strength to the view that the roots of that style are Asiatic. When the Sarmatian phase was well advanced a sword with a ring pommel came into use; it has its counterpart in China under the Han dynasty, and it appeared in late Roman Hungary.

The summary of the story tells of a period of intense activity in the steppes from the Carpathians to Turkestan and eventually to China. In an early phase there was intercourse with Anatolia and the Caucasus region for iron, together with possible relations with Greek or pre-Greek maritime adventurers; this phase is also linked up with Cimmerian conquerors or rulers, whose origin is not clear. Later, Scythian invaders with an Asiatic background, akin to that of the Iranians, dominated the scene for some centuries and were neighbours to the Greek colonists in south Russia. They in turn gave way before the Sarmatians, who were still more Asiatic and whose movements are somehow related to those which put the Chinese Empire in touch with the West and prepared the way for trade across Asia.

BOOKS

HERODOTUS. *Histories.*
MINNS, E. H. *Scythians and Greeks* (Cambridge, 1913).
ROSTOVTZEFF, M. *Iranians and Greeks in S. Russia* (Oxford, 1923).
DALTON, O. M. *The Treasure of the Oxus* (B.M. London, 1926).
BOROVKA, G. O. *Scythian Art* (London, 1928).
PARVAN, V. *Dacia* (Cambridge, 1928).
CHILDE, V. G. *The Danube in Prehistory* (Oxford, 1929).

2

An Attempted Recovery in the Riverine Lands of the Near East

THE fall of the Cretan power in the fourteenth century, and of the 19th Dynasty in Egypt and the Hittite rule in Anatolia in the thirteenth, involved changes in the positions and activities of the peoples in the south-west of Asia and Egypt. The iron for which the Hittites had become famous was doubtless an object of envy and strife, and Woolley has described the effects of invasions of barbarians with iron weapons, perhaps ultimately from the northern grasslands, at the old trading city of Carchemish. These fastened their clothes with *fibulae*, made coarse pots with geometric ornament, burned their dead, and built fortifications in a much more scientific fashion than did any of their predecessors. The Amorites or Amurru of north Syria, on the other hand, seem to have fallen before Aramaean tribes sweeping in from the desert border, and these peoples gave to the Syrian area languages that lasted for many centuries. Both Babylonia and Egypt were weak, and the trade of Crete fell into the hands of merchants of Tyre and Sidon, whose efforts form the subject of Chapter 3.

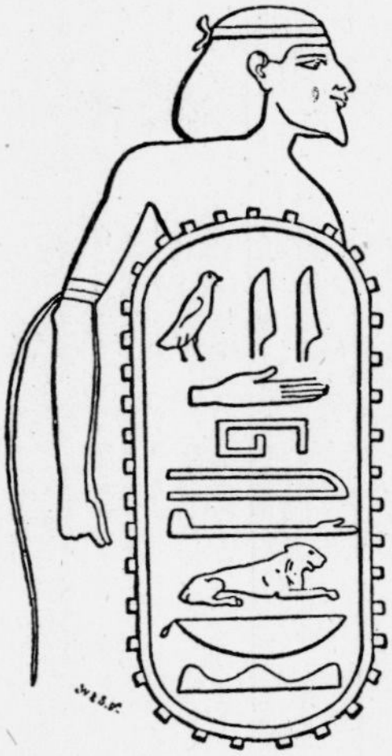

The economic decline in Egypt left the country under priestly rule; she ceased from exporting manufactured goods through Mediterranean middlemen, and came to depend on her peasantry, who were providers of grain on a considerable scale. A few incidents of Egyptian life during the next centuries may be mentioned in passing. Sheshonk, the Shishak of the Old Testament, set himself up as the first king of the 22nd Dynasty in 945 B.C., and took advantage of the quarrel between the northern and southern elements of the Hebrews after the death of Solomon to attack Jerusalem, whence he brought back booty about 930 B.C. The weakness of Egypt is, however, revealed by the fact that Osorkon was beaten by Asa, king of Judah, in 895 B.C. The story continues to be one of decline until the conquest of the Delta by Esarhaddon of Assyria in 671 B.C.

FIG. 6. Figure recording the conquest of Judaea by Shishak.

In south-western Asia the new setting of the scene, and the spread of the use of the horse, led to the rise of Assyria in the north of Mesopotamia as described in Chapter 5 of *The Horse and the Sword*. This power was in the main crude and barbaric, though Tiglath-pileser I does seem to have done something for the economic organization of Assyria itself; conquered lands were merely sources of plunder or of tribute. After Tiglath-pileser's death in 1102 B.C., the external possessions of Assyria fell away until Adad-nirari, who was king from 912 to 889 B.C., extended its sway once more and followed his defeat of Nabu-shum-ishkur, king of Babylon, by a treaty demarcating their frontiers. Tukulti-ninurta, who reigned from 889 to 884 B.C., started a series of annual campaigns, which were continued by his successors for nearly sixty years. Between 884 and 869 B.C. Ashur-nasir-pal developed Assyrian power, and Sangara, a prince of Hittite extraction, who had become ruler of Carchemish, paid him a tribute of gold, silver, bronze, and iron, as well as ivory, doubtless imported from Africa, and woven woollen mantles. The horse and the chariot, siege-engines in the form of towers on wheels equipped with battering-rams, and companies of archers are the features of the military equipment of the time. Incredible barbarities accompanied these conquests. From this period come the earliest bas-relief picture records of Assyrian history.

In 859 B.C. Shalmaneser III succeeded his father, and in 849 B.C. he took Carchemish and reduced it to the position of an Assyrian colony. In 841 B.C. he attacked Hazael, king of Damascus, and, though not at first completely successful, by 837 B.C. he had taken all his cities and levied tribute on Tyre, Sidon, and Byblos. Two of the finest works of Assyrian art belong to this time. The bronze bands found at Balawat are decorated in repoussé work with scenes representing the most notable campaigns of this monarch, while the famous black obelisk contains twenty small reliefs, depicting similar scenes and processions of captives.

Shalmaneser's son, Shamshi-Adad V, who reigned from 824 to 811 B.C., led his army right round his kingdom to ensure the loyalty of the outlying tribes, after which he proceeded north into the land of the Nairis, which lay around Lake Urmia. Then he destroyed 1,200 towns or villages of the Medes, an Iranian

tribe that had lately settled in this region and of whom we shall
hear more as we proceed. Lastly he marched from the mountains to the shores of the Mediterranean to make certain of the
good behaviour of his Syrian subjects. Two years later, in 818
B.C., a war broke out between the Assyrians and Marduk-
balatsu-ikbi, the king of Babylon. This was waged fiercely for
nearly eight years, until in 811 B.C. Shamshi-Adad took the city
of Babylon and died shortly afterwards, when he was succeeded
by his son Adad-nirari III.

Adad-nirari seems to have been a minor at his accession, for
until 808 B.C. his vast domains were governed, and well governed,
by his mother Samru-remat, better known to us as Semiramis
and credited with attempts at religious reform tending towards
monotheism. A few years later the king concluded a treaty with
the king of Babylon, thereby defining the boundary between the
two kingdoms.

Adad-nirari was succeeded in 782 B.C. by his son Shalmaneser
IV, who was to meet with greater troubles than his immediate
predecessors, for a new power was arising in the north and was
bent on disputing his authority in that quarter. This new
power was the kingdom of Urartu, formed, it would appear, by
a small band of steppe people, who had imposed their rule upon
the Anatolian inhabitants of the region around Lake Van.
Between 781 and 774 B.C. Shalmaneser was engaged in a number
of campaigns against the rulers of Urartu, and was usually unsuc-
cessful, so that ultimately his boundaries in this direction were
forced southwards. In the end his power was so weakened that
the Syrian states began a revolt, which he was quite unable to
check. For a time the power of Assyria appeared to be waning,
and in 772 B.C. Shalmaneser died and was succeeded by his son
Ashur-dan III. Almost from his accession the new monarch
suffered a series of disasters, for all his northern subjects were
taken from him one by one by the king of Urartu. This loss of

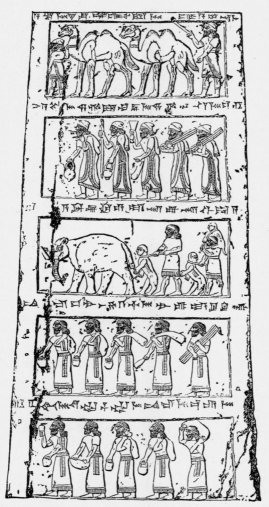

Fig. 7. Black obelisk of Shalmaneser II.

territory led to a serious diminution of trade, unemployment followed, and a number of the more populous cities in his dominion revolted between 763 and 758 B.C. Though he was eventually successful in restoring order, it was a sadly diminished kingdom that, on his death in 751 B.C., he left to his son Ashur-nirari V. This monarch, the last of his line, was totally unable to restore order. Matters went from bad to worse, until in 746 B.C. Kalakh, the capital, revolted and the king perished.

After an interval of a year a man arose who was to restore the fortunes of Assyria. This was Tiglath-pileser III, who assumed the crown in 745 B.C. This king was not of the royal line, but has been thought by some to have been a general named Pul. By 742 B.C. he had restored peace on his borders and two years later he subdued Babylonia, where he left Nabonassar in charge. He pressed back the frontiers of Urartu, then erected a number of fortified posts among the Medes to keep these marauders in check. Lastly he marched into Syria, where he met Sarduris, king of Urartu, whom he defeated in Commagene. In 737 B.C. he extended his dominions to the north and attacked Sarduris in his capital at Van; though he set up a monument before the gates of that city, he failed to conquer the country. In 735 B.C. he attacked Syria, and the following year marched through Palestine as far as Gaza; in 733 B.C. he took the cities of Damascus and Samaria, and deported much of the population of Israel and other neighbouring groups. In 728 B.C. he took Babylon, and at his death in 727 B.C. he had extended his kingdom from the Persian Gulf to Mt. Demavend and along the eastern Mediterranean coast to the borders of Egypt. During his reign he built a great palace at Kalakh, with gateways and a colonnade in the Hittite style.

Shalmaneser V, who succeeded him, was probably his son. He extended his kingdom into Cilicia, but soon afterwards Hosea, king of Israel, rebelled and carried on an intrigue with the king

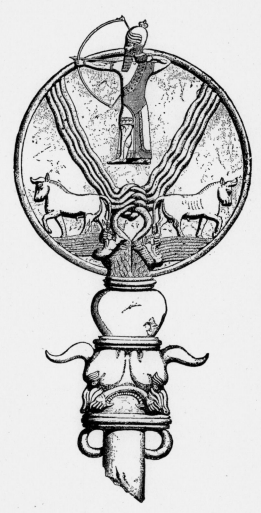

Fig. 8. Sargon's standard, with figure of Ashur.

of Egypt. Shalmaneser besieged him in Samaria for three years, but died in 722 B.C. before it fell.

At the death of Shalmaneser V a new dynasty was founded by Sargon II, who was probably a descendant of earlier kings. He had not long been on the throne when Merodach-baladan, in alliance with Khumbangash, king of Elam, entered Babylon and threw off the Assyrian yoke. Sargon had other troubles on his borders, but he surmounted them, and in 710 B.C. took away the northern half of Babylonia from Merodach-baladan, deposing that monarch and installing his own son, Sennacherib, as governor in 709 B.C. After defeating Urartu he attacked the Cimmerians in 705 B.C., and defeated them, but fell in battle. Though most of his reign had been taken up with repeated campaigns to retain his territory intact, he found time to build a new city, Dur-Sharrukin, the modern Khorsabad.

Sargon was succeeded by his son Sennacherib, who spent the first two years of his reign in rebuilding Nineveh, in which he erected a magnificent palace, lined with processional friezes in alabaster. Later on he had to police his western possessions from Syria to Palestine, and to reduce to subjection Hezekiah, king of Judaea, who had been encouraging others to revolt. He laid siege to Jerusalem but was unable to take it, though he succeeded in causing Hezekiah to submit and to become a tributary prince. Most of his time, however, was spent in peaceful avocations, erecting fine buildings, executing great engineering projects, and improving the state of agriculture by introducing several new plants, including cotton. His beneficent reign was brought to an end in 681 B.C. by a sad tragedy, for he was murdered by his two sons, who did not succeed him, for a third son, Esarhaddon, then reigned in his stead.

Esarhaddon, like his father, was king of both Assyria and Babylonia, and was paramount lord of most of the lands in southwestern Asia. Like his father, too, he was content to hold the kingdom he had inherited without farther extensions, but on more than one occasion he was compelled to quell disorders on his borders or to put down revolts. In 679 B.C. the Cimmerians, driven on by some Scythian tribes that had crossed the Caucasus, made raids upon the Assyrian frontiers, though these were easily repelled by the provincial governors with their local forces. In 675 B.C. Taharka, king of Upper Egypt, endeavoured to persuade Ba'alu, king of Tyre, the only independent state left in that part of Asia, to attack the Assyrians. Esarhaddon obtained early information of this intrigue and set out without delay for the Egyptian frontier, and during the next year he began to reduce the fortresses in the Delta, while in 673 B.C. he started to besiege the city of Tyre. Making little headway in these undertakings he withdrew to organize greater preparations, and in 671 B.C. he conquered Egypt. Two years later he paid a visit to that country to set the place in order, and while there fell sick and died.

Esarhaddon was succeeded on the throne of Assyria by his son Ashurbanipal, while another son, Shamash-shum-ukin, became ruler in Babylon under his brother. Ashurbanipal had scarcely ascended the throne when the people of Upper Egypt claimed their independence and drove out the Assyrian governors, but in 607 B.C. these re-established their rule, and in 664 B.C. Necho, prince of Sais, was placed in command of the Delta, and his son Psamatik made governor of Athribis. On the death of Necho in 663 B.C. Psamatik succeeded as governor, and between 658 and 651 B.C. contrived to clear the Assyrian garrisons out of the country. The siege of Tyre was raised soon after the accession of Ashurbanipal, who concluded a treaty with Ba'alu.

About 653 B.C. Shamash-shum-ukin, finding that most of his Chaldean subjects intensely disliked the Assyrian overlordship, and fearing that he might lose his position at Babylon if he acquiesced in the suzerainty of his brother, plotted with the Elamites and other neighbouring peoples to throw off his allegiance to Ashurbanipal. A revolt broke out in 652 B.C., but the Assyrians, after a campaign of four years, took Babylon in 648 B.C. and brought the whole country again under their rule. Shamash-shum-ukin, who had been deposed in 650 B.C., died in 647 B.C., and his place at Babylon was taken by Kandalanu. Little is known of the events of the last few years of Ashurbanipal's reign, except that he died in 626 B.C.

Like his immediate predecessors, Ashurbanipal was essentially a peaceful king and led or sent his armies only to defend his frontiers and to put down revolts and intrigues. Like others of his house he was a great builder and erected a fine palace, the decorations from which enrich our great museum. In this palace, unlike his predecessors, he formed a large library, in which he collected a great assortment of books in the form of clay tablets. Some of these had probably come down from an earlier date, but most of them seem to have been inscribed for the purpose of the library. A number of these works were in Sumerian and other early tongues, and that they might be understood it became necessary to provide dictionaries and grammars. It was the discovery of this library by Layard in 1848, with its stores of literature, both ancient and modern, dealing with contemporary affairs as well as with history, religion, and folk-lore, that has enabled scholars to decipher not only the Assyrian but also the Sumerian and other languages, thus restoring a great many pages in the history of the land between the rivers.

At his death in 626 B.C. Ashurbanipal was succeeded in turn by Ashur-etil-ilani, and Sin-shan-ishkar, who reigned until in 610 B.C. Nineveh was attacked and taken by the Medes in conjunction with Nabopolassar, who had made himself king of Babylon; the city was destroyed and its inhabitants fled to Harran, where they lived undisturbed until Nabopolassar attacked them and attempted to drive them out. Later he found

FIG. 9. Ashurbanipal crossing a river.

himself opposed by the Syrians, who were in alliance with Necho, king of Egypt, and after some fruitless fighting he died in 605 B.C., when he was succeeded by his elder son, Nebuchadrezzar.

It is partly because the remains of some Assyrian cities were the first to be discovered and excavated by the pioneers of Near-Eastern archaeology, and still more because of the wealth of sculptured panels that lined the walls of their palaces, that the Assyrian kings have acquired a disproportionate fame among students of ancient history. Some of the Assyrian monarchs were, it is true, great generals and administrators, and their soldiers were well-disciplined and sturdy warriors, not averse from acts of ruthlessness when their leaders desired it. The wealth that followed upon their many conquests enabled these kings to build magnificent palaces, lined with innumerable sculptured friezes, that now enrich our museums. Nevertheless, their contributions to the advance of civilization were slight. They kept back for a time the advance of those Iranian tribes that were later to dominate great parts of Asia, so that, when it came to their turn to conquer, they were less barbarous than, we may suppose, they had been some centuries earlier. For this, doubtless, we may be grateful, but the chief value of these Assyrian monarchs in the eyes of the historian is that two of them at least formed great libraries of books written on imperishable clay, and have thus opened to us not only pages but volumes of the history of the past that must otherwise have been lost past recall.

Before returning to Egypt to witness another attempted revival and the final downfall of that power, we must devote a few lines to the kingdom of Urartu, to which reference has more than once been made. It would seem that in or before the ninth century B.C. a group of men, allied to the Mitanni, and therefore presumably from the northern grasslands, had brought under their rule the inhabitants of the mountain region surrounding Lake Van. We first hear of them in 859 B.C. and again in 855 B.C., when there is mention of Arame, a king of Urartu, who seems to have had his capital at Arzaskur. About 840 B.C. Sarduris, the son of Lutipris, founded the city of Van on the shores of the lake, and called himself king of the Nairi. He, it would appear, was the real founder of the kingdom known to the Assyrians as that of Urartu and to the Hebrews as Ararat.

The kingdom of Urartu at first occupied the region on the east and south-east sides of Lake Van, though it was subsequently extended to cover the greater part of Armenia. The people of this country used a form of Asianic speech, and their rulers did not, as in other cases, introduce into this any element of their own Indo-European tongue, from which we may gather that the noble class was relatively small. Sarduris I seems to have been succeeded by his son Ispuinis, of whom little is known, but his son and successor, Menuas, who was ruling the kingdom about 810 B.C., greatly extended its boundaries. Menuas associated his son, Inuspuas, with him on the throne, but the latter seems to have died before his father, who was succeeded by Argistis I, who still farther enlarged the kingdom, as did his son and successor Sarduris II. In 736 B.C., however, Tiglath-pileser II, king of Assyria, resenting these enlargements on the south, attacked Sarduris and besieged his capital, and, though the Assyrian was not successful in taking the city, Sarduris died shortly afterwards, when he was succeeded by a son Uedipris, who took the name of Rusas.

Since the Assyrians were determined to reduce the extent of his kingdom, Rusas I allied himself with the Mita and the Muski, both of which peoples were under the rule of chieftains whose ancestors had come originally from the northern grasslands. In spite of this alliance Rusas was defeated in 714 B.C. by Sargon, and shortly afterwards committed suicide. During the reign of his son and successor Argistis II the land was ravaged by Cimmerians and Scythians, while Phrygians, displaced by these, annexed the western half of the kingdom. Matters went from bad to worse under his son and grandson, Rusas II and Sarduris III, till at length the kingdom of Urartu became absorbed by the Medes and ultimately included in the Persian empire.

We must now return to Egypt. Esarhaddon, the king of Assyria, had conquered the Delta in 671 B.C., and had made the Theban kingdom a tributary province. As we have seen, in 664 B.C. Ashurbanipal appointed Necho, prince of Sais, as governor in the Delta, in which post he was succeeded at his death the following year by his son Psamatik, who, between 658 and 651 B.C., drove out the Assyrian troops and made himself independent monarch of Lower Egypt, thus founding the 26th Dynasty.

It would appear that since the close of the eighth century, if not earlier, there had been a Greek settlement near Sais. This had been founded by traders from Miletus and was at first called the 'Fort of the Milesians', though it was later known as Naucratis. Necho, the prince of Sais, a chieftain of Libyan origin, was helpful to these traders and to others settled at another fort known as Daphnae; and Psamatik, his son, continued on excellent terms with these merchants, and traded with them to their mutual advantage.

For some time Psamatik ruled only in the Delta, but by degrees his influence reached higher and higher up the river; at length in 655 B.C. he allowed his daughter, Nitocris, to be adopted by the high-priestess at Thebes, and opinion in that city was satisfied. From 650 B.C. he was considered the undisputed monarch of the whole country.

Between 630 and 625 B.C. the Scythian hordes ravaged the whole of south-west Asia as far as Palestine, where they founded a city. To check their advance Psamatik built a series of forts along his frontier, garrisoning them with mercenaries recruited from his Greek friends at Naucratis, and thus succeeded in keeping these wild hordes out of his domain.

Even after he had dismissed the foreign garrisons, Psamatik remained very friendly to the kings of Assyria, and especially to Ashurbanipal, to whose help he came on several occasions during that monarch's dissensions with Babylonia. For the most part,

Fig. 10. Bas-reliefs, time of Psamatik I.

however, he remained within the boundaries of his own kingdom, engaged on peaceable tasks, until his death in 609 B.C.

His successor was his son Necho, who continued his father's policy of friendship with the Assyrians, who had by this time been driven out of Nineveh and had taken refuge in Harran. Here they were being attacked by Nabopolassar, king of Babylon, when Necho immediately after his accession came to their assistance. The following year he set out again to help his friends to recover Harran, which had been captured by the Scythians, and on the way defeated Josiah, king of Judaea, who had come out to oppose his passage, at the pass of Megiddo, the scene of so many battles ancient and modern. These struggles brought him into direct conflict with the king of Babylon, whose son Nebuchadrezzar drove him back to his own land. Since he had now lost all his outside possessions, he engaged in more peaceable undertakings, such as the construction or repair of the canal to the Red Sea, while he dispatched a fleet to circumnavigate Africa, a voyage that was brought to a successful conclusion.

After his defeat of Necho, Nebuchadrezzar succeeded his father as king of Babylon, inheriting an empire as extensive as that of Assyria in its palmiest days. In 597 B.C. Jehoiakim, king of Judah, rebelled, and Nebuchadrezzar besieged Jerusalem. During the siege Jehoiakim died and was succeeded by his son Jehoiachin, after which the city fell and the Babylonian monarch appointed Zedekiah to be tributary king of the land.

In 593 B.C. Necho died and was succeeded by his son Psamatik II, who in 591 B.C. paid a ceremonial visit in great state to the Phoenician cities, which had up to now retained their independence. He died in 588 B.C., when he was succeeded by his son, known to the Greeks as Apries and to the Jews as Hophra. This king encouraged Zedekiah, king of Judaea, to revolt against the king of Babylon, who in 587 B.C. besieged and took Jerusalem, captured and blinded its king, and carried off its inhabitants into captivity. Apries, like his predecessors, was on excellent terms with the Greeks at Naucratis, and began to adopt Greek customs; this so annoyed the Egyptian nobles that they would have deposed him, had it not been sacrilege to lay hands upon the anointed of Ra. Instead they appointed Amasis, the leading general, as co-regent, and Apries was kept virtually a prisoner until in 566 B.C. he escaped, revolted, and was killed.

Amasis began his reign by asserting his authority over the Greek traders; he compelled them to abandon Daphnae, so that all of them could live in Naucratis. Later, however, he fell a victim to their charms, and married a Greek lady from Cyrene, by the name of Ladice. He abstained from increasing his territories in the north-east, but during his reign the Greek colony became tributary, while Cyprus submitted to his rule.

Nebuchadrezzar was now becoming an old man and too infirm to lead armies abroad; also all serious opposition to his rule had died down. He spent his remaining years in completing the fine buildings with which he had been adorning Babylon, such as his magnificent palace with its hanging garden, numerous temples, and the fine Ishtar Gate; he also restored the Great Processional Way. At length he died in 562 B.C., when he was succeeded by his son Amel-Marduk, known to the Jews as Evil-Merodach.

Evil-Merodach seems to have been an unpopular monarch, and after two years of ineffective rule he was deposed in 560 B.C. by Neriglissar, who had married his sister, and who is believed to have been the true heir to the earlier dynasty of kings. He died in 556 B.C., when he was succeeded by his son Labaki-Marduk; he was deposed the same year by the priests, who appointed Nabonidus as king of Babylon in his place. Nabonidus was a scholar and a gentleman, but not distinguished as a general, and during the latter part of his reign disorders began to develop, due partly to his inactivity but largely to the folly and conceit of his son Belshazzar. About 547 B.C. Cyrus, who had become king of the Persians, began to encroach upon his boundaries, and yearly filched away part of his possessions. The writing had already appeared upon the wall, and in 539 B.C., having changed the course of the river, Cyrus entered Babylon.

Thus all that had belonged to the great Assyrian empire, and had later been ruled by the omnipotent Nebuchadrezzar, passed into the hands of Cyrus the Persian, who became indeed the king of kings. The days of Egypt were also numbered, although its independence outlived the great Iranian conqueror. Amasis died in 527 B.C., when he was succeeded by his son Psamatik III, who had scarcely reigned for a year when in 526 B.C. Cambyses, the decadent son of the great Cyrus, marched across the desert and conquered the land of the Nile, which never again until our own day succeeded in regaining its independence.

BOOKS

Cambridge Ancient History, vol. iii (Cambridge, 1925).
OLMSTEAD, A. T. *A History of Assyria* (New York, 1923).
SMITH, SYDNEY. *A History of Assyria* (London, 1927).
BREASTED, J. H. *A History of Egypt* (New York, 1912).

3

Maritime Traders in the Great Sea

DURING the greater part of the Bronze Age the main bulk of the maritime traffic in the Near East was in the hands of the inhabitants of the Isles of the Aegean, as we have seen in earlier volumes of this series, especially in *The Way of the Sea* and *Merchant Venturers in Bronze*. It is true that the second city of Hissarlik had a considerable foreign trade, but this was largely by overland routes, though some of its wares reached the West by a line of traffic that set out from the head of the Gulf of Corinth. Towards the end of the third millennium this maritime traffic came more and more into the hands of the merchant princes of Crete, who retained almost a monopoly of this commerce until the destruction of Knossos and of the other great cities in Crete about 1400 B.C.

After this great catastrophe the commercial centre moved to the mainland of Greece, and Argos, Tiryns, and Mycenae in the Peloponnese, as well as Thebes and other centres north of the Isthmus, grew rich on this overseas traffic. By degrees, however, most of these cities came under the rule of Achaean chieftains, many of them, it is thought, of Phrygian origin, and, as we have seen in *The Horse and the Sword*, these heroes were more intent on marauding expeditions than on the peaceful avocations of trade; maritime commerce in their hands became scarcely distinguishable from piracy. Under the rule of the House of Atreus in the Peloponnese most of the traders of Minoan origin, now apparently distinguished from the other inhabitants as Ionians, crossed the isthmus into Attica, while many of these ultimately found a home and suitable bases for their maritime adventures upon the shores of Asia Minor and its adjacent islands.

The years immediately preceding and following 1200 B.C. were fateful for the great empires in the Near East. The Kassite Dynasty at Babylon fell in 1196 B.C.; the Hittite Empire came to an end shortly before under the repeated attacks of invading hordes of Phrygians, while in 1205 B.C. the 19th Dynasty in Egypt, under whose government the welfare of that country had been decaying with great rapidity, passed on the rule to a rapacious priesthood that kept the whole population in servitude. Then came the great campaign before the gates of Troy, not only leading to the capture and destruction of that citadel, but leaving the victors so impoverished of leaders and resources that, after two generations of ineffectual rule, the Achaean power gave way before the incoming Dorians. All trade in Aegean waters seems to have come to an end for a time, for little was produced and the population had become too poor to provide a profitable market.

It was under these circumstances that the eastern coast of the Levant, no longer a cockpit between contending Egyptian and Hittite forces, showed signs of activity. Saul established

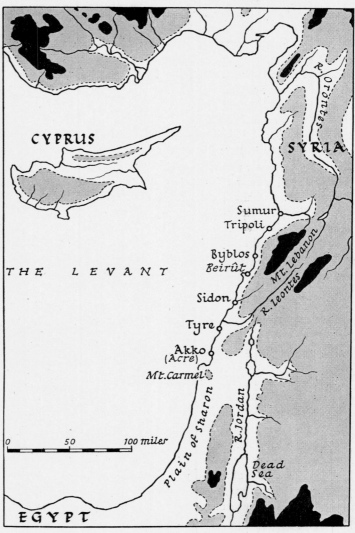

Fig. 11. Map of Phoenicia.

a kingdom, uniting the Hebrew tribes against Philistine aggression; David expanded this realm to include the fertile Plain of Sharon, hitherto occupied by the Philistines, while Solomon encouraged trade and reaped the benefit of sitting across two important trade routes.

It was at this time that a new commercial power came upon the scene; it was destined to hold a leading place in the world's trade for nearly a thousand years. The name Phoenician seems to have been used in earlier days by the Achaeans and other Hellenes to denote the sun-tanned seamen of the Aegean, and appears to have been especially applied to the Cretans, for Cadmus was traditionally spoken of as a Phoenician, yet he was a cousin of Minos and brought the Cretan linear syllabary to Boeotia. In the period following the Trojan War the name gradually became attached to the merchants from Tyre and Sidon and other ports on the Syrian coast, and these are the people known by that name in historic times.

Phoenicia thus played a great part in the life of the world early in the last millennium B.C. It was essentially a series of harbour-cities along the Syrian coast north of Mount Carmel and the Bay of Acre. These cities stood on peninsulas or on islets in several cases, and the coastal plain behind them is narrow, since the forested mountains of Lebanon rise almost immediately behind it, and from these large numbers of winter torrents rush down to the sea. The most southerly city is Akko, the later Acre, at the north corner of the bay of that name, and thence Phoenicia stretches northwards to the region within reach of the Orontes basin, communicating easily with the interior, but open to Hittite influence.

The study of the archaeology of Phoenicia is still at an early stage of development, though there has been great progress in the last ten years. The region south of the Litany or Leontes river in the early second millennium seems to have been

Canaanitish, while that farther north, beneath the Lebanon itself, was, to some extent at least, Amorite. Byblos has yielded evidence of Copper Age culture, and, as early as the time of the 3rd Dynasty, ships, known by a Canaanite name interpreted as Byblos-farers, carried cargoes of cedar wood and other things to Egypt. There are also indications in the records of Sargon I that about 2700 B.C. Mesopotamia was already interested in the cedars of Lebanon and in Mediterranean trade. It thus seems safe to say that the region afterwards known as Phoenicia was a participant in the general spread of commercial and civic activities of the early part of the third millennium B.C.

Royal tombs dating from the first half of the second millennium B.C. show strong Egyptian influence. There are also many references to Phoenicia on Egyptian monuments of the Middle Kingdom and the early days of the Empire. The Amarna letters give abundant indications of the fears of the people of Phoenicia when Egyptian power was weakening in the later days of the 18th Dynasty. The Phoenician cities which were specially affected in this way were those which lay north of the promontory of Beirut. Farther south, Sidon was already important, and, to judge from archaeological evidence of about that time, in touch with Aegean or Mycenean culture, while Tyre had already begun its important career. Hittite pressure broke the political relations between Egypt and northern Phoenicia, leaving the more Canaanite south still under Egyptian protection for a while, but in the end Egypt lost all. It would seem a useful, if very tentative, hypothesis that this phase led the south to have greater importance than it had had of old. In early days, apparently, Sumur, not very far north of Tripolis, had been a leading city with a Pharaonic palace, while Byblos and a number of towns in the next large coastal concavity were also powerful. The Amarna letters show Sidon rebelling against

Egypt, and it became a leading city for a while, but, when Phoenicia's enlarged opportunities came, the primacy passed to Tyre. The Hebrews long used the name of Sidonians for their northern neighbours; for later periods prophetic denunciations such as those in chapters xxvii and xxviii of Ezekiel are mines of detailed information.

The opportunities of Phoenicia, as of Israel, were enlarged when the Hittite Empire had fallen; Egypt was weak, and Assyria, the rising power in the Mesopotamian region, was not yet strong enough to demand more than occasional gifts. In Phoenicia, however, there is a background of ancient trade relations, contacts, and mixings of peoples, whereas the Davidic effort in Israel is, politically and commercially, a minor affair in a region farther from the centres of business life that was just emerging from the barbarism portrayed in the books of Joshua and Judges in the Old Testament.

That the peoples of the Phoenician cities spoke a Semitic language and are depicted on Egyptian monuments with Semitic features should not be taken to imply that they and their commercial culture are all of Semitic origin. Long-standing intercourse over wide areas must have meant much admixture, and at any rate Hittite, Amorite, and Canaanite elements from near by would be present; none of these were Semitic, but were probably Semitized in language, especially in the south, which became the more important region when Sidon, and still more when Tyre, took the lead. Like other groups of trading cities, the Phoenician ports were evidently jealous of one another, and associations were often loose and fluctuating. Another feature was that little effort was made to acquire a wide territory behind the cities; it was evidently deemed best to conclude agreements such as those made between Hiram of Tyre and Solomon. It is noteworthy that only in much later Hellenistic times did a sea-deity come to be worshipped in

Phoenicia; the earlier gods are related to hills and springs, trees and rivers, and suggest a peasant folk. Each district has also its deity with the title of king or queen of the city. The goddess-queen of Byblos gradually became likened to Hathor of the

Egyptians, the influence from each people working on the other. The god Melek, Milk, Molech, or Moloch, like many others, was served with human sacrifices in times of crisis. The god of Tyre was named Melqarth, apparently meaning simply 'king'; he was the local Ba'al or Bel. The goddess-queen of Byblos was Ishtar, the Ashtoreth of the Old Testament, Astarte being the Greek form of this name. Eventually Greek mythological names tended to replace the early ones, but it has been claimed that, through Cyprus and Sicily, the Phoenicians exercised a large influence over the development of Greek religion.

FIG. 12. Terra-cotta figure of Ashtoreth.

In the last part of the second millennium B.C. not only were the Phoenician cities without Egyptian, Hittite, or Mesopotamian overlordship, they also had special maritime opportunities after the breakdown of the Minoan-Mycenean commerce, and their influence in the Aegean appears to have begun in the twelfth century B.C. In due course the Phoenician cities, especially Tyre, founded a number of colonies, but, since merchants from Greece, Ionians and Aeolians for the most part, had made many settlements on the coast of Asia Minor, the Phoenicians confined their westward efforts to an extension of their Egyptian voyages along the African coast and to Sicily and Malta, eventually spreading also to the Iberian peninsula. The Phoenicians were ultimately pressed back by the Greeks, but long held the western end of Sicily.

For understanding the details of their later development, it is of importance to realize that their efforts in the eastern half of the Great Sea obviously met with serious obstacles.

Meanwhile, at home the cities were feeling the expanding power of Assyria, to which they paid tribute from time to time. Sidon was annihilated after a rebellion about 678 B.C. Tyre also had previously revolted in conjunction with Sidon, but on its island site it managed to hold out. When Assyria was breaking down, Egypt's power flickered up in an attempt, defeated at Carchemish in 605 B.C., to take the Phoenician ports. Thenceforward for a time they felt the power of Babylon, and Tyre withstood a siege of thirteen years from Nebuchadrezzar between 585 and 573 B.C. before it surrendered on terms which apparently protected it from plunder. Under the Persians a revived Sidon, on the mainland, took the lead from Tyre. Alexander the Great was welcomed in most Phoenician cities, but not at Tyre, so he laid siege to it, and drove the famous mole across from the mainland to the island fortress to carry his engines of war. With the help of the other cities and the Cypriotes he took Tyre in 332 B.C, and his foundation of Alexandria finally helped to reduce the trade of Phoenicia.

The cities, though often nominally subject to Egypt, Assyria, Babylon, or Alexander in the course of their history, were, nevertheless, of great value to these overlords for purposes of trade and transport. They distributed the products of the lands around, and the prophet Ezekiel, in chapter xxvii, gives a remarkable picture of their trade relations. Cedars of Lebanon and oaks of Bashan, ivory brought by way of the isles of Chittim, sometimes said to be Cyprus, fine linen and embroidered work from Egypt, blue and purple from Elishah, thought by many to be the Gulf of Laconia, silver, iron, tin, and lead from Tarshish, in south Spain, horses from Togarmah or western Armenia, horns of ivory and ebony and fine clothes brought

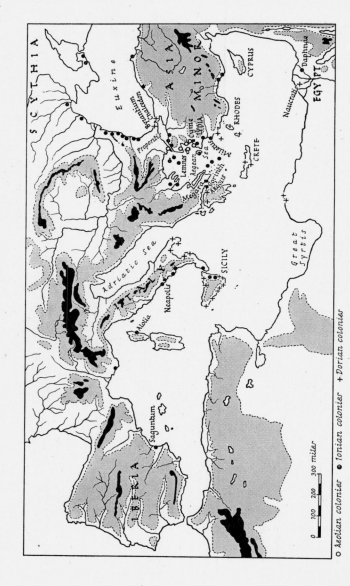

FIG. 13. Map showing the distribution of the Greek colonies.

from Dedan, which may have been the Hejaz, wheat from Minnith, east of Jordan, honey, oil, and balm from Israel and Judah, wine and wool from Damascus, lambs and goats from Arabia, spices and precious stones and gold from Sheba, slaves and brass from Javan or the Aegean, Tubal, and Meschech on the south-eastern coasts of the Black Sea—all these and much more came through Tyrian markets. Mercenaries from Persia, Lud, in the west of Assyria, Phut, perhaps the African coast opposite Sheba, and merchants from all around contributed to the greatness of Tyre. Tarshish was of very special importance, and one may trace the spread of the Phoenicians westwards to that rich source of metals probably about the end of the second millennium B.C. The traditional date of the foundation of Carthage as a colony of Tyre is 813 B.C., and it seems that the value of Tarshish was a main factor in encouraging the coloniza- tion which developed in the western Mediterranean, with Malta and western Sicily as centres of special importance.

The Tyrian colonies paid tribute to Melqarth, the god-king of the mother city, and were at first under the city's rule. Probably as early as the ninth or tenth century the Dorians competed with the Tyrians in Greek lands; the taking of Cyprus by the Assyrians in the eighth century interfered for a while with the control of valuable sources of timber and copper. Soon afterwards the Greeks began to make themselves felt in the western Mediterranean and Tyre's political power waned, while by the sixth century Carthage was asserting her independence.

The Cassiterides or Tin Isles, mentioned in connexion with Phoenician voyages to the west, have been a subject of endless discussion, and, among other places, isles off north-west Spain, isles off the south coast of Brittany, and the Scilly Isles have been suggested. There is no ground for any confident conclusion at present.

North-west of Phoenicia trade was mainly in the hands of the Greek cities and their colonies. Many of the latter had been founded, as we saw in *The Horse and the Sword*, by refugees from the mainland who were unwilling to tolerate the Dorian usurpation. These colonists were, for the most part, the descendants of the earlier pre-Hellenic population. The Aeolians, who went from Thessaly to plant colonies on the coast of Asia Minor and the adjacent islands, from Cyme to the Hellespont, were probably descendants of the First-Thessalian immigrants, reinforced by those of the invaders that had introduced the Dhimini culture. Ionians spread farther afield into the Aegean, the Propontis, and the Euxine, where people from Miletus settled on the northern shore in close proximity to the Scythian tribes of south Russia. They also colonized the north-east corner of Sicily, and eventually spread over the northern coast of the western Mediterranean, from near Massalia to Saguntum on the east coast of Spain, having half-way houses at Alalia in Corsica and around Naples. They also established settlements on the southern coast of Asia Minor and had two depots in Egypt, to which reference has already been made; one of these, at Naucratis, was later eclipsed by Alexandria. These colonists, as we saw in *The Horse and the Sword*, represented what was left of the Cretan settlers in the Peloponnese, and in a great measure their trading activities were in the regions that had formerly done business with Knossos. The Achaean colonies are more puzzling. The colonists seem to have been of mixed origin, but mainly descendants of the earlier inhabitants of the southern coast of the Gulf of Corinth, who had been engaged during the latter half of the third millennium in the trade from the head of that gulf to south Italy and still farther west, as described in *The Steppe and the Sown*. It is not surprising, therefore, to find that the main group of their colonies was in the toe of Italy. Another series in Cyprus was probably of different origin, and dates not so much from the period of early trade as from the time of the sea-raiders.

Lastly, there were the Dorian colonies. These can hardly have been founded by the true Dorians, who were a fighting and a pastoral people who despised trade and even in their own land left commerce in the hands of foreign settlers called Perioeci. Most of these colonies were founded from Corinth, which, though nominally a Dorian city, was peopled to a great extent by descendants of the population that had gathered at the head of the gulf in the great trading days of the third millennium. The Dorian colonies were for the most part on either side of the mouth of the Adriatic, on the coasts of which no settlements were made, since little was to be gained there by way of trade. There were also a number in the south of Sicily and on the north coast of Africa, to the east of the Great Syrtis. In the seventh century the people of Megara founded a colony at Chalcedon, which had apparently continued the trade that was formerly in Trojan hands, and a little later on the far more defensible site at Byzantium. Thus they held most of the really strategic positions, such as the entry to the Adriatic, across which trade to the west had to pass, the Bosphorus, guarding the entrance to the Euxine, as well as Crete and Rhodes, which commanded the southern exits from the Aegean.

Though, as seems likely, these colonists were descendants of the pre-Hellenic settlers in Greece, they all spoke the Hellenic language and followed the Hellenic religion; not only did they consider themselves Hellenes, but, in later days at least, were firmly convinced that they were descendants of Hellen, as can be read in the pages of Thucydides. The Hellenic language belongs to the Indo-European linguistic group, which, so we have argued, arose in the grasslands of south Russia and Turkestan. Nevertheless, it had absorbed a number of features from the tongues of the earlier peoples, some grammatical usages and certain words, especially those connected with the soil, such as the names of some trees and plants, as well as of the earthworm and the mouse.

The official Hellenic religion was still more composite and clearly the result of a concordat, by which all the deities formerly worshipped had been admitted to Olympus, under the kingship of Zeus, the sky-god of the grasslands, who had ousted Cronos, the former chief deity, from his pre-eminent position, and had banished to Tartarus those that failed to fit the new scheme. One deity, of the early metal-workers, was admitted to the Olympian halls but found to be incongruous there, so Hephaestos was cast out and fell on to the island of Lemnos, where he remained, permanently lamed from his fall. The mother goddess of Asia Minor, worshipped by the First-Thessalians, by the Cycladic folk, and by most of the Cretans, adopted a Hellenic name and was known as Demeter, though her mate, Tammuz, was converted into a daughter, Persephone. The sea-going Cretan element retained Poseidon as ruler of the waters, while another primitive deity, Dis, claimed the underworld of Hades. Hesiod, in his *Theogony*, elaborated this concordat and established relationship between Zeus and the other denizens of Olympus. Finally, the Hellenic people celebrated this amalgamation every fourth year at the Olympic games, which took place in the Peloponnese at Olympia, where Zeus, the Indo-European deity, had been married to Hera, who, despite her Indo-European name, was a goddess, probably of Cretan extraction, who had been worshipped since Mycenean times at her shrine, the Heroon, in the Plain of Argolis.

The Greek colonies were not, however, the sole traders, either in the Aegean or in the west, during the whole of the period under review in this volume. When the Hittite Empire fell before the Phrygians about 1200 B.C., the trading activities of the people of Asia Minor came to an abrupt end, for the

Phrygians preferred commercial isolation and, if we interpret correctly the story of Midas, were wont to hoard their gold. Trade among the Hittites had been to a great extent in the hands of colonies of Sumerian merchants, much of whose commercial correspondence on baked clay tablets has come to light in recent years, as has been described in previous volumes of this series. With the arrival of the Phrygians these commercial activities of the Sumerians must have come to an end, and we may conjecture that they deserted their old homes and looked for settlements elsewhere. Though we have no certain evidence on this matter, it seems probable that they moved westwards into the land of the Maeonians, which formed part of the eastern border of the Aegean Sea.

If we may trust the legends related by Herodotus, it was not long after the destruction of the Hittite Empire that a chieftain called Agron, who claimed descent from Heracles, and who is thought by some to have been of Indo-European origin, made himself master of the Maeonians, whom his dynasty ruled until 685 B.C. as kings of Lydia. It was, according to Herodotus, a generation or two before the arrival of Agron that, owing, he says, to a scarcity of corn, some of the inhabitants of this country decided to emigrate; they assembled at Smyrna, embarked with their families and worldly goods, and set off to found settlements elsewhere. Some of these, in whom we may perhaps recognize the remnant of the commercial communities of the Hittite Empire, seem to have settled for a while in Lemnos, where an inscription has been found which appears to have been left by them; others were living at a later date in Thrace not far from Crestona, while the majority set sail for the west, where, as Tyrrhenians, they built towns in the territory of the Ombrici. These Tyrrhenians, better known as Etruscans, were established in their new home in Italy by 800 B.C., if not earlier, and here they founded about eighteen cities, each the centre of a small state, the states being linked together into a confederacy. Each of these city-states was governed by a magistrate, who was to some extent a leader in religion, and was known as a Lucumo. It is interesting in this connexion to remember that the Sumerians in Mesopotamia had lived in city-states, each governed by a religious magistrate known as a Patesi. Moreover, both peoples were given to the practice of hepatoscopy, or divining the future by inspecting the liver of a sheep. It can scarcely be a coincidence that the only three known models of a sheep's liver, marked out in regions for the guidance of the augurs, come, one from Mesopotamia, probably from the temple of Marduk at Babylon, the second from Boghaz Keui, the Hittite capital, where there was a colony of Sumerian traders, and the third from near Piacenza, in north Italy.

It was about 700 B.C. that a native of Sardis, which had now become the capital of Lydia, discovered that there was gold in the sands of the Pactolus, which flowed beneath the city. This discovery was made, apparently, by one of the king's bodyguard, Gugu, known to the Greeks as Gyges, and according to Herodotus a son of Dascylus. Gyges doubtless grew rich from the proceeds of his new-found gold-field, and at length so influential in Sardis that he became its ruler. We need not necessarily place implicit trust in the scandal related by Herodotus and repeated by Cicero, but there is no doubt that about 685 B.C. Gyges succeeded Candaules, the last Heraclid, as king of Lydia, founding the dynasty known as the Mermnadae.

It has been suggested that Gyges was a Heraclid noble; this we think is unlikely. His accession to power inaugurated a new phase in Lydian policy, and the country became at once a commercial centre. This suggests that the new king came of a mercantile family. After his accession Gyges, unlike the Phrygian monarchs, desired to make his newly-found gold serviceable as currency in the interests of foreign trade. Hitherto, trading had

a

b

Fig. 14. Models of sheeps' livers from (*a*) Babylon and from (*b*) near Piacenza.

been by barter, and the precious metals had been exchanged for commodities by weight. The gold native to the Aegean region is found mixed with a variable amount of silver, an alloy known as *electrum*, and this caused much confusion in business transac-

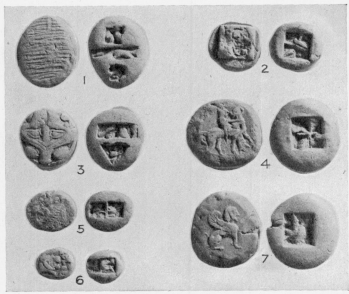

FIG. 15. Early electrum coins from Asia Minor.

tions. It is said that Gyges was the first to purify the gold by removing its silver content and so to produce a metal of standard purity. The masses so purified needed a standard mark, and this was supplied by striking the lump on an anvil with a hammer on which a design had been cut. It was found convenient, also, to guarantee the weight as well as the purity of the metal, and when this had been done and marked with a stroke of the hammer, a token had been made of such a reliable standard that it could be used as a common counter for trade in every market. Thus, it has been believed, came about the first use of coins, and thus arose the first gold currency.

Such was the generally accepted legend as to the origin of coinage, but recent study has given reasons for qualifying this statement. It is true that the earliest coin known to have been issued by a king bears stamped upon it a lion's head, which is known to have been the badge of the Mermnadae, the royal house founded by Gyges. Nevertheless, a large number of coins of a simpler type have been found, for the most part in Ionian cities, and it has been suggested by Milne that these were struck by Ionian merchant-bankers two centuries or more before the usurpation of Gyges.

Professor Ure has argued with great skill that the introduction of coinage into the Aegean world, thereby bringing in a new type of values, gave a great advantage to the abler traders over their less skilful colleagues brought up to the practice of barter. This caused the rise of a limited number of men of great wealth and acuteness, who by degrees obtained absolute power in their states. Thus many of the Greek colonies, all of which had in the beginning been governed by a privileged class, came under the rule of tyrants, supported by the populace, and those that had done so increased in wealth faster than their neighbours. Be this as it may, it is an undoubted fact that the rise of a gold currency was accompanied in many cases by the transfer of absolute power into the hands of a few individuals, and it may be but a coincidence that analogous changes seem to be attending its abandonment.

After the introduction of the coinage, trade improved rapidly in Lydia under the descendants of Gyges, who ruled the land as tyrants, a name of Lydian origin. Gyges was followed in turn by Ardys, Sadyattes, Alyattes, and Croesus, each tyrant growing richer than his predecessor, till the wealth of Croesus became proverbial. This last of the Lydian tyrants, who rose to power in 560 B.C., extended his dominions from the Aegean to the Halys, and made all the Greek colonies in that region his tributaries. He considered himself the most fortunate of men, and he is reported to have said so to Solon, who was visiting his court at Sardis. To this the sage is said to have replied, 'Call no man happy until he is dead', words that Croesus had cause to remember on a later and tragic occasion.

BOOKS

Cambridge Ancient History, vols. ii and iii (Cambridge, 1925).
MILNE, J. G. *Greek Coinage* (Oxford, 1931).
RANDALL-MacIVER, D. *Villanovans and Early Etruscans* (Oxford, 1924).
URE, P. N. *The Origin of Tyranny* (Cambridge, 1922).

4

Israel

IN Chapter 6 of the last volume of this series, *The Horse and the Sword*, the survey of the Near East in the twelfth century B.C. included a reference to the waning of the previously dominant influence of Egyptian culture in Palestine. The Phoenicians had profited by the downfall of Crete to spread their trade in the Red Sea and the Mediterranean, though their colonies in the West are of later date. The Philistines, migrants who had occupied the south part of the coastal plain of Palestine after moving from the south of Asia Minor, were dominating Palestine. They were developing varying relations with the Hebrews, who, under Joshua, had occupied the highland around Mount Ephraim and parts of the country rising west of what was later known as the Sea of Galilee, as well as of the hills east of Jordan, between the river Yarmuk and the Dead Sea. This group of Hebrews is often called the Joseph group. Its people were largely herdsmen and had entered into relations with a Caleb group in the hills of what was later known as Judah. That highland still, however, remained in large measure outside the Hebrew tradition, and in it the sacred fortress of Jerusalem and the sister fortress at Gezer farther west were of great importance. Much of the higher surface here was wilderness with small patches of relatively fertile land supporting little fortified towns. Some have thought that this pre-Israelite element in the south may have been people cherishing the traditions of Abram and of the Law, which, in its Old Testament form, is known to include an early edition of the same set of ideas as were built up in Mesopotamia into the code of Hammurabi and elsewhere into analogous codes. The Law of the Pentateuch, however, includes sections of very various dates, edited some centuries after the period now under discussion; Exodus xxxiv, for example, is related to the life of a settled peasantry.

The central feature of the Hebrew people or Israel is the linking of a number of peoples by the acceptance of the law and ritual as a covenant between the god Jahweh and the people. They are a confederation, obviously a loose one at first, as we may judge from the Song of Deborah, one of the oldest fragments of the Hebrew tradition, and from the famous Shibboleth story. That song makes no reference to the Philistines and may well date from a time before they dominated the country. The song also suggests that the people entered into a covenant with Jahweh in the wilderness, at the Mount of God, somewhere south of Edom; that covenant is the basis of the group's life and gives possibilities of new adhesions to the confederation.

Not only the fortress cities of the later Judah, but also the lowland of Esdraelon or Jezreel, were in the possession of non-Hebrews, and it is probable that the fortress at Bethshean was in Canaanite-Egyptian hands until the Philistines took it.

In the book of Judges the Hebrew tribes act for the most part

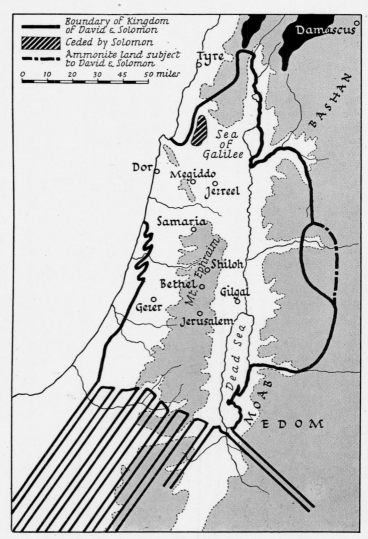

FIG. 16. Map showing the Kingdoms of David and Solomon.

as buffers between the more settled peoples and the Moabites, Midianites, Ammonites, and others coming across Jordan westwards, probably moving in successive groups from the wilderness towards the sown land during the period of hot, dry climatic conditions occurring about 1400–1200 B.C., which we discussed in *The Horse and the Sword*. It is natural that, in the course of their efforts, Hebrews mingled with the people they were often protecting, and sometimes doubtless attacking; the consequent admixture of ritual is an abundant subject of comment in the book of Judges. Towards the end of that book Israel figures no longer as a fighter amongst equals, but as a rather barbarous people in contact with more civilized Philistines. A new situation had by this time arisen and was to lead to great changes in the life of Israel. The culminating point of the Philistine power came when Shiloh and the ark were taken by the Philistines, and no smith was allowed by them in the land lest Israel should make swords or spears. Whether Israel previously had any quantity of such weapons and was deprived of them, or whether this episode represents diversities of culture levels, need not be argued here; nor need it be more than suggested that the presence of a powerful common enemy and the destruction of the old sacred place at Shiloh were enough to cause the people of the covenant of Jahweh to seek a military leader and a more permanent organization to face the foe. This is the main factor in the rise of the kingship, which at first clearly concerned the central or Mount Ephraim group, including the Benjamites, of whose efforts under Saul, about 1025–1015 B.C., the first book of Samuel gives an account, describing alternating victories and defeats. It is when the southern group comes into the struggle, under David, that the situation changes. He is the central figure in the history of Israel, and he almost makes the people one. Eventually he set a seal on his achievements by the capture of Jerusalem, a centre of ancient sanctity from pre-Israelite times, making its appeal to the people of the south as well as, during David's lifetime, to the group around Mount Ephraim and in a measure to the group east of Jordan, though these still hankered after the lineage of Saul. David must have been well versed in the traditions of Jahweh and held his leadership as a covenant, now tripartite, between Jahweh, himself, and the people. The Philistine strength was meanwhile declining, Egypt under priestly rule had lost its aggressive power, the Hittite Empire had broken down, and neither Assyria nor Babylon had at this time the strength to make conquests in the west. The Phoenicians seem to have been anxious rather to ensure the safety of their trade through the interior than to make conquests, so Israel under David was able to build itself up and came to be a nation looking to Jerusalem, which, under Solomon, was made the centre of the worship of Jahweh, symbolized by the ark in the Temple.

Solomon clearly sought to convert the kingship from the covenanted basis approved by David to one of absolute power like so many other kingships of antiquity in south-western Asia; his exactions for the building of palaces and temples must have drained the resources of his subjects severely. Moreover, realizing his position in the midst of potential enemies, he contracted marriage-alliances that involved the setting up of the various cults of his queens side by side with the ritual of Jahweh and the priesthood that was growing around it in Jerusalem. Though this arrangement might foreshadow later attempts at toleration under Cyrus and under the Romans, it could hardly be acceptable to those who believed that theirs was the only true worship in the land of the Hebrews. For a time a measure of success attended this effort, and Solomon directed trade with ships on the Red Sea, brought gold from Ophir, had visitors from Sheba with spices and precious stones, and organized caravans of horses carrying linen from Egypt, while chariots were also used. He had an understanding with Tyre and may have accepted the ruler of Egypt as an overlord. There was in fact an effort to transcend traditional barriers and to work out a larger scheme in commerce, politics, and religion. The death of Solomon is placed round about 933 B.C., and then the internal weaknesses of Israel became apparent very rapidly. Alt has argued very recently that, even in the time of David, the Hebrew peoples of the centre and north merely acknowledged his political and military leadership, and that the unity was only a personal affair. Even if this needs qualification, there seems little doubt that the Palestinian groups, whether urban or rural, had a good deal of the localism so conspicuous, for example, in Greek life, and lacked the concept of the larger unit that was a feature in Egypt, where the authority of the Pharaoh of the whole land was accepted and maintained over long periods, even if there were occasional relapses into sectionalism. The story of the split between the southern people, now including Judah and Benjamin as well, the latter probably because of proximity to Jerusalem and the ark in the temple, shows that Jeroboam, the leader of the centre and the north, found it necessary to emphasize another emblem of Jahweh. He used the emblem of the bull-calf worshipped in the ancient holy place of Bethel by the people of the centre and in Dan by the people of the north. Shiloh did not reappear, and the ark had now gone to the southern group, but Jeroboam's scheme was obviously not planned as apostasy to Jahweh, on whom the northern and central peoples had closer claim than the southerners.

It is obvious that the people of the central and northern groups were becoming in large measure settled farmers, and that capitalism and its attendant luxury in high places were growing fast. Here was far more arable land than it was possible to develop in the wild southern hills. Moreover, the way through Jezreel from Megiddo and Dor to Bethshean and the Jordan was a highway of trade from Egypt to Bashan, Damascus, and the Euphrates; so Jeroboam's kingdom was far more in touch with the world in general than was the little highland remnant that clung to the house of David in Jerusalem. Jeroboam was, apparently, under Egyptian influence, and Sheshonk of Egypt made himself overlord of the south as well. The opportunity for a large-scale power in Palestine, based upon the strong and sacred fortress of Jerusalem, had gone by; for, even if Egypt was on the whole declining, Assyria was developing westward aggression.

The increased importance of settled cultivation with every man under his own vine and his own fig-tree, in place of the old life of the rude herdsmen, may in a measure be interpreted in terms of cultural evolution. The herdsmen, in the days of the Judges, having on the whole protected the cultivators, learned from them, and, with progress of intermarriage, acquired items of equipment and comfort, and were no doubt inclined to accept the Baal cults of the cultivators as increasingly more suitable to their new circumstances than the rude cult of Jahweh traditionally associated with old wild days of herding nomadism. Another supplementary line of interpretation is, however, suggested by the fact of a widespread change at this time, affecting Europe and Mediterranean lands, to a moister cooler climate. Less burning aridity in summer would favour cultivation in Palestine, and would give the country relative freedom from nomad raids, as well as increase the importance of trade routes and stations, such as Damascus, on the way to and from Mesopotamia.

Whatever the causes, it is, at any rate, clear that the northern and central peoples in Israel were entering more into the general life of their time; they were somewhat inclined to look upon the tradition and ritual of Jahweh as a relic of old and barbarous days when it had led them to slay those neighbours from whom they had now learned so many of the arts of civilization, and whose blood, through many intermarriages, now flowed in their

FIG. 17. Carved ivories from Samaria.

veins. At the same time, there was the almost inevitable change
from a people with the democratic feeling of the desert-border,
modified by acceptance of the personal influence of a leader, to
a peasantry under an aristocracy of wealth and extortion gathered
around the palace of a monarch impelled by circumstances
towards despotism. Partially gilded ivories inlaid with coloured
paste have recently been found at Samaria and date from the
time of Ahab and Jezebel, but, curiously, are Syrian rather than
Phoenician. There is a striking contrast between this and the
old spirit of comradeship and a common loyalty to the ritual
and covenant of Jahweh. The Hebrews, under David, had come
nearer to the achievement of a national unity on that old basis
than any known people appears to have done; that is probably
one reason why the ancient tradition showed such vitality, and
sought expression in other ways when the political sphere no
longer offered adequate opportunities. Robinson has recently
suggested that the failure of David's grandson, Rehoboam, to
maintain the Davidic unity, already imperilled by luxury, ex-
travagant schemes, and maladministration under Solomon, was
a factor of great importance in turning the minds of the tradi-
tionalists towards cultural and ethical ideals, and so in shaping
the great religious and literary contribution that the Hebrew
people were to make to the life of the world.

The central and northern peoples evidently did not take
easily to the idea of a despotic monarch, and were unsettled by
their contacts with other peoples and other rituals, as well as by
the internal conflict between the worship of Baal and that of
Jahweh, the latter cut off from the influence of the priestly
group that had grown up around the temple at Jerusalem; this
made a regular dynastic succession difficult to maintain. One
usurper after another became king, and external alliances varied
from time to time, while there was little understanding of the
growing power of Assyria. Of the kings who followed Jeroboam

we know that Omri and Jeroboam II gained widespread power
and showed considerable skill, but the kingdom was too small,
and the openness of the plain of Jezreel made it too easy to
penetrate. Moreover, as we shall see in reference to Persia,
engineering skill was advancing rapidly with special development
of means of communication, and politics of the traditional
Israelite kind were now out of date as well as incompatible with
the need for fusion with perhaps both Damascus and Tyre.

Fig. 18. Part of first face of black obelisk of Shalmaneser, with Jehu doing
obeisance.

Moab asserted its independence against Omri's son Ahab, and
Damascus sometimes claimed privileges and even overlordship,
though it became subject to Ahab for a time, while that same king
obviously regarded the king of Judah as, in some respects, his vassal.

The southern group in the hills of Judah had as sources of
unity the ancient tradition of sanctity of the fortress of Jerusalem, enriched by the possession of the ark and by the activities
of the priestly body. It may have been the influence of the
priests, as well as the lingering power of the Davidic tradition,
that kept the kingship in the historic family, and avoided the
great number of revolutions and usurpations that were such
a feature at Samaria. If, in addition, the code of law was largely
a heritage of the southern element, this was another factor
of a certain stability. Further, invasion was difficult. A king of
Judah might, therefore, accept in times of stress a position of
subordination to some outside power, knowing full well that he
could act more or less as he chose. The people of the south were,

therefore, less inclined to religious syncretism, that is the simultaneous practice of many rites belonging to the gods of different peoples, as well as more conservative; but there are many indications that the conservative view found expression in the centre and north as well.

Groups like the Rechabites condemned the drinking of wine; it was a feature of the settled life, to which they opposed their idea of inhabiting tents such as the early Israelites had used. The Nazarites were obviously another conservative group. A further expression of the same feeling was to become far more important to the world.

A very old feature of religious life in south-west Asia had, apparently, been the occurrence of people who showed evidences of mental excitement, as we have shown in Chapter 3 of *The Horse and the Sword*, and gathered in bands known as sons of the prophets or seers. Whether from among these, or side by side with them, there arose later the more definite prophets, these at any rate owed to the tradition of their predecessors the possibility of a recognition, even by kings, of their spiritual prestige. With a basis in tradition, they very naturally sought to maintain the worship of Jahweh, and some think they were concerned with loyalty to the Davidic tradition that was maintaining itself in the Temple at Jerusalem. They were unofficial and irresponsible teachers moving about amongst the common people, as one gathers from the story of Elisha, and they naturally became critics of the court, of luxury, and despotism, and often of foreign alliances. Amos, one of the early prophets, gives a picture of very distressed conditions and irresponsible violence in the eighth century B.C., and he refers in a hostile spirit to the ceremonial at Bethel and Gilgal and to the need for justice and mercy to the poor. He denounces the beds of ivory, the music-making, and the wine-drinking, and suggests the bitter days that are coming when the people shall be led captive. For him, Jahweh is not only the god of Israel but the almighty creator of the whole universe. Micah denounces violence and greed, scant measure and wicked balances, the priests that teach for hire and the prophets that divine for money; and he looks forward to the day when many nations shall come to worship Jahweh and a Messiah shall deliver his people. Joel, on the other hand, is more particularly the religious patriot. Hosea, eager for justice and mercy, at the same time has his attachment to Jerusalem rather than to Bethel and Gilgal, to the Davidic tradition rather than to the bull-calf emblem of Jahweh. The first section of Isaiah, which includes chapters i–xxxix, has parts which belong to the same general period. It often appears, from incidental remarks, that whatever the faults of the priests at Jerusalem, those that gathered at Bethel and the other places of the Jeroboam tradition were an unorganized rabble much mixed up with the adepts of other cults; it has already been argued that the central and northern Israelites were hardly in a situation to develop a pure tradition of their own. They were definitely conquered and led captive in large numbers by the Assyrians after the middle of the eighth century B.C., but the southern group lingered on for more than 100 years, and this made much of the surviving Hebrew tradition, of whatever origin, cling around Jerusalem. None the less, it must not be forgotten that a very small community, no doubt very mixed, claims to have persisted in Samaria right down to our own day. The invasion of Sennacherib in 701 B.C. maimed Judah severely; it was henceforth for some time subject to Assyria. Jeremiah, the prophet of the end of the seventh century, carries on the tradition of the exclusive demands of Jahweh, but sees that the old ritual is not enough; he has a vision of a spiritual deity and of personal and individual relations of his people with him. In his day came the fall of Assyria and the rise of Babylon to supremacy, and he appears to have advised submission to Babylon before the final extinction of the kingdom of Judah through the Babylonian captivity. Like his predecessor, Isaiah, he saw the weakness of Egypt as well as the degradation of his own people, and it is characteristic of his insight that his hopes for the future were centred upon the exiles taken to Babylon rather than upon the remnant left at Jerusalem.

The rise of the prophets is the great feature of the life of Israel, and the high artistic quality and power of thought and diction among them is an indication of what the human mind was becoming able to do under the stimulus of a great anxiety and of the breakdown of a system that had been handed down by tradition. The early prophets such as Elijah and Elisha are remembered as wonder-workers, around whom stories have grown among the common people; the later prophets are literary giants, leading the thought of their people from the narrow limits of the old covenant and ritual to the idea of a universal God, whom some of them as yet barely apprehended, and who must be served less through a ritual than through righteousness of life. Ezekiel sees that Babylon will scourge not only the Jews who are not faithful exclusively to Jahweh, but also Tyre and Egypt. In chapter xlvii he says that Jerusalem is to be a holy centre. The priestly group in Jerusalem meanwhile codified the ancient covenant as a reformed Law written in what is preserved as the book of Deuteronomy, which many scholars ascribe to the reign of Josiah, who was king of Judah between 639 and 608 B.C., though there are difficulties in accepting this view. The records of the kings, or parts of them, were put together not long afterwards.

It is, therefore, easy to understand that the priestly and prophetic traditions, combined more particularly in Ezekiel, were handed down especially, though not entirely, through Judah, while it has already been suggested that, on the other hand, the northern group, or Israel, melted away in captivity under Assyria.

The power of Assyria began to decline before the middle of the seventh century B.C., Nineveh itself falling before the Babylonians and the Medes in 612 B.C.; it was during the period of the decline of Nineveh that Josiah and his priests revived the old rites at Jerusalem and apparently codified the law and the records of the kings. Babylon, under Chaldean rule, took the leadership from Assyria, and at Carchemish in 605 B.C. inflicted a crushing defeat on Egypt, which had made efforts to revive its influence in and beyond Palestine as Assyria weakened. Judah was for some years between the two powers, but in 586 B.C. Jerusalem was captured by Nebuchadrezzar and many of the leaders were taken to Babylon; some, including Ezekiel the prophet, had been taken thither in 597 B.C. Babylon, in its turn, fell before Cyrus, the Persian, in 539 B.C. and a new era began.

Cyrus was disposed to encourage Hebrew and other regional cults and to allow their followers to regulate their lives accordingly, subject to the acceptance of his supremacy. He was willing to be a king of kings rather than always and everywhere a single and despotic ruler and, in pursuance of this policy, he allowed Hebrew, or as one may by this time say, Jewish exiles to return to Jerusalem. Having had the codified law and the reformed ritual of Josiah's time in trust in their keeping, these exiles had naturally remained distinct and apparently had prospered in Babylon. With the return of some of them from exile comes the third great literary outburst exemplified in the second half of Isaiah from chapter xl onwards, with its clearer concept of a God of the whole universe and of a traditional covenant between Jahweh and the Hebrew people. After the return of the exiles from Babylon under Cyrus, conflict arose between the tradition re-established at Jerusalem and that persisting among the remnant of the Samaritans, and an account of this period by apologists for the Jerusalem rites is given in the books of Ezra and Nehemiah. The prophetic tradition lived on, and the later part of the book of Zechariah includes a vision of Jerusalem as the religious centre for the whole world. The idea of a Messiah or deliverer became very widespread.

In the Hebrew scriptures we thus have a vivid and highly artistic account of the development of religion from a stage in which a tribal god, Jahweh, was worshipped by means of traditional rites to one in which God is envisaged as the Creator and Sustainer of the Universe, the Arbiter of Fate, and the Personification of Righteousness. Abstract thought liberated itself from the foundation of tradition and began to wing its own way; the Babylonian captivity had widened the Jewish vision and given it a universalist tinge, however much the attachment to Jerusalem might limit this and encourage priestly influences towards emphasis on correctness of ritual and the old tradition. There was, in fact, a marked growth of the historic sense as an accompaniment of the increase of range of thought.

As an addendum to the main theme of this chapter, it should be stated that the Hebrew scriptures give reference to new invaders of the later part of the seventh century B.C., who are identified by many scholars with the Scythians discussed in Chapter 1.

BOOKS

SMITH, G. A. *The Historical Geography of the Holy Land* (London, 1910); *with Atlas* (London, 1915).
ROBINSON, T. H. *A History of Israel* (Oxford, 1932).

5

Law and Philosophy in Greece

THE downfall of so many kingdoms, as described in our last volume, *The Horse and the Sword*, and the arrival of barbaric invaders in many lands, especially in Greece and Asia Minor, led to profound changes in the organization and outlook of the inhabitants of these areas. The old tribal organizations required remodelling, the old tribal deities were no longer felt to be supreme, nor were the old rituals sufficient to secure the safety and prosperity of the nation. The people became reorganized, no longer on a kinship but on a territorial basis, indigenous tribal gods in some regions became associated with the deities of the invaders to form a hierarchy, in others they gave way to heroes by the apotheosis of a famous leader of a former generation, while in others again, though the gods were not disowned, the intellectuals became interested less in theology than in philosophy.

On the Greek mainland, where the fusion between the aborigines and the invaders was more complete, the tendency to substitute a regional for a kinship basis came about slowly, as codes of laws began to supersede tribal custom. These laws, however, are in marked contrast with those drawn up in Judaea, where the book of Deuteronomy was being compiled about this time, and where emphasis was laid upon duty to a personal God, whose influence extended beyond tribal boundaries. On the mainland the hierarchy of Olympus became the official object of worship, though greater honour was often paid to a hero who was believed to have been connected with the city. In times of emergency the people had recourse to the oracle at Delphi, originally, it is thought, of Cretan foundation, though at this time believed to be under the inspiration of Apollo.

In the colonies, especially in those on the Asiatic coast of the Aegean, tribal organization had perished at the time of the migration, and was retained in name only in the Ionian cities. Here organization was by cities, and the laws, it would appear, were mainly commercial codes. Since the people of these cities held frequent intercourse with traders from outside the Greek world, the traditional religion decayed more rapidly, and, instead of

implicit belief in the Olympic hierarchy, or the reverence for
heroes, the more leisured inhabitants, especially in the Ionian
cities, turned their thoughts to speculations as to the origin
of things, and evolved a philosophy on a definitely evolutionary
basis, in this feature resembling some of those arising in India
and to a less degree in China.

The legends relating the story of the Dorian conquest tell us
that the Peloponnese was taken by the three sons of Aristo-
machus, whose names have come down to us as Temenus,
Aristodemus, and Cresphontes. According to these accounts
they reached the peninsula across the Gulf of Corinth, sailing
from Naupactus, where Aristodemus is said by some authorities
to have died. Having conquered most of the Peloponnese,
except the mountainous country of Arcadia in the centre, they
divided between them the territories they had annexed; of these
Temenus received Argolis, Laconia went to the twin sons of
Aristodemus, while Messenia is said to have fallen to Cresphontes. This last statement appears to be erroneous, though
it seems likely that the third group of Dorians acquired some
lands in the west of the peninsula.

After the coming of the Dorians and the destruction of the
Mycenean civilization, each district in Greece, as we saw in *The
Horse and the Sword*, took to making pottery after its own traditional method, and a variety of wares, decorated with geometric
designs, grew up in every area. In Attica the bulk of this pottery
was made at the Ceramicus, just outside the Dipylon gate of
Athens. Here the pots made grew larger and larger until some
of colossal size were produced. In addition to the geometrical
designs, there were bands surrounding the vases on which were
depicted funeral processions of men and chariots and horses, all
drawn in black on a buff ground in a highly stylized manner.

The geometric wares provided for the needs of most parts of
Greece until, soon after 750 B.C., a new ware began to develop

Fig. 19. Dipylon ware.

in Sicyon, and by 730 B.C. to be carried to all the colonies in the west. This ware, which is known as Proto-Corinthian, consists of beautiful pear-shaped *lekithi*, decorated sometimes with processions of animals. It was followed shortly afterwards, about 700 B.C., by the Corinthian ware, usually of a buff paste, heavily decorated in purple paint with designs believed to have been introduced from the east, where they had been used for embroidery. About the same time the Dipylon ware gradually gave way to the Phaleric, made at Phaleron, one of the ports of Athens. The Corinthian ware soon captured the monopoly of the western market, while the Phaleric was mainly used for home consumption, but before 600 B.C. the artists at the Ceramicus developed their graceful black-figured vases, decorated with beautifully drawn figures in black on a smooth red ground, and during the sixth century this ware superseded the Corinthian and was extensively exported to Etruria. After the Persian wars, beginning in 490 B.C., the Attic potters developed a new style of decoration, painting a black background and allowing the figures to stand out in red, so that fine detail could be painted upon them. This red-figured ware lasted in use for a long time, and was carried all over the Mediterranean area; it was copied in south Italy, especially in Apulia, where the style, much degenerated, lasted almost down to the beginning of the Christian era.

A few words must be said here about the development of architecture during these centuries, though it will be impossible to give an adequate account of this great subject in the space at our command. It will be remembered that in the second chapter of an earlier volume of this series, *Peasants and Potters*, we described the evolution of the log cabin as one of the first types of dwelling to be used. By allowing the side logs and the roof timbers to project beyond one of the end walls of such a cabin, a porch would be formed to protect the entrance. Evidence of the existence of such dwellings, as early as the third

a

b

c

d

FIG. 20. Greek vases: *a*, Proto-Corinthian; *b*, Corinthian;
c, Black-figure; *d*, Red-figure.

millennium, has been cited from Transylvania and from the Second City of Hissarlik. Homer describes the house of Odysseus as such a dwelling, which is known as a *megaron*. We can realize that in larger structures of this type it would be found convenient to place a beam upon the top logs, and then to fill in the space above to support the projecting roof; but to keep this beam from sagging a number of upright wooden posts, planted in the ground, would be needed. Thus apparently arose the columns surmounted by a pediment that are found at the ends of Greek temples. Since such temples consisted of two independent chambers, opening at each end, surviving from the time when dwellings had two compartments, one for men and the other for beasts, the columns and pediments are found at both ends of most temples. A further elaboration was to allow the rafters to overhang considerably, then to support the ends of these on beams, which in their turn were held up by rows of posts. This became the peristyle which is such a frequent feature in the more important Greek temples.

In this way, when the wooden structure had become translated into marble, arose the Doric temple, the form usually found in Greece and in the majority of the colonies, and at an early date the pediment was found to be a convenient space for decoration, which had become most elaborate by the sixth century B.C. In the Ionian cities the architecture became most ornate, and the plain Doric columns gave way to the more elaborate Ionic columns with their voluted capitals. At a still later date developed the Corinthian columns, with their capitals of carved acanthus leaves.

There is little doubt that the first important settlement of the Dorians had its capital at Argos and included the whole of the eastern part of the Peloponnese and the adjoining islands. The Kingdom of Laconia, with its capital at Sparta, was, it is thought, founded some generations later by invaders from Argolis, and became from the beginning an independent monarchy. By degrees it grew more powerful than its eastern neighbour, and at times annexed some of the richer parts of southern Argolis, but in the seventh century there arose a king who, for a time, redressed the balance. This was Pheidon, whose date is variously given by different authorities, but who seems to have been at

FIG. 21. A Doric temple.

the height of his power in 668 B.C. He succeeded in restoring to his kingdom all that had belonged to his ancestor Temenus, except the city of Corinth, with its surrounding lands, which had long been under the rule of independent kings and was now governed by an oligarchy, the Bachids, drawn from the descendants of one of these monarchs. At Pheidon's death, which is said to have occurred while attempting to take Corinth, the kingdom passed to his son Lacedes, who appears to have been a weak ruler. The kingdom, so carefully restored by his father, fell to pieces, all the cities, which had been growing rich by oversea trade and were now issuing their own coinage, declared their independence, and soon after 660 B.C. most of them, according to the fashion of the time, placed themselves under the rule of tyrants, a name borrowed from the Lydians, over whom Gyges had lately established the earliest tyranny.

Sparta, almost alone among Greek states, remained under the rule of its two kings, reputed descendants of the twin sons of Aristodemus. Their authority was somewhat qualified by the power of the nobles, the descendants of the original Dorian conquerors, who formed a close aristocracy. These Dorians lived under a traditional tribal law, and governed with no little severity the descendants of the Mycenaean traders, known as Perioeci, and those of the earlier Helladic settlers, who, as Helots, were reduced to a condition of serfdom and tilled the land for their masters. The Spartan nobles conquered Messenia, which seems up till then to have been free from Dorian rule, and they reduced its inhabitants to a state of serfdom even more severe than that which they had placed upon the Helots. The Messenians ultimately protested, but to no avail, and between 650 and 600 B.C. they revolted, unsuccessfully, against their lords.

After putting down the Messenian revolt the Spartans reconsidered their position. They were now a privileged aristocracy ruling a vast number of unwilling, and in some cases rebellious, serfs. Their position was not secure, and they felt it necessary to reorganize themselves the better to be able to keep these unruly elements in subjection. They adopted, therefore, a scheme of organization known as the Eunomia, which at a later time was attributed to Lycurgus. Whether the scheme was indeed drawn up by a law-giver of that name is uncertain, for no reliable details of his life have come down to us; it seems more likely that the laws, having been drawn up and adopted by the Spartan nobles, and modelled on some customs already in use in Crete, were placed under the protection of a deceased hero of that name.

It was, it would appear, about 600 B.C. that the Eunomia came into force. The three Dorian tribes into which the Spartan

nobility had been divided were abolished, thereby bringing to
an end the ancient tribal customs that had hitherto governed
the behaviour of the nobles. In their place were established five
new tribes, tribes only in name and not in constitution, which
had no longer a family but a territorial basis, for their names
were taken from the four quarters of the town of Sparta and from
Amyclae, the older settlement, now, to all intents and purposes,
a suburb. In these so-called tribes were included not only those
of strict Dorian descent, but also such others as had sufficient land
to support them without any labour on their own part, so that
they could give their whole time to the service of the state. All
the members of these tribes, which were in reality regiments,
formed part of the army of the state. All were considered equal,
and all had to lead a life of Spartan simplicity. In actual fact,
however, all were not political equals, for those of true Dorian
descent alone had certain religious privileges, and they alone
were eligible for appointment as members of the Gerousia, or
Council of Old Men.

The state under this constitution was governed by the
Gerousia, consisting of the two kings and twenty-eight Gerontes,
and by the Apella, a body consisting of all the members of the
tribes. It would appear that no business could be initiated
except by the Gerousia, and that the members of the Apella
were called upon only to vote on it, and could, apparently, be
dismissed if the majority disagreed with the more august body.
The protection of the opinions of the larger body was entrusted
to five Ephors, one from each tribe, a fresh duty placed upon
a body of officers that had existed for some other purpose before
the adoption of the Eunomia.

This is not the place to describe in detail the rules of Spartan
discipline, of the upbringing of their boys and the separation of
the sexes for meals, for this subject has been amply treated on
many occasions. At first, after the adoption of the Eunomia the

Spartans traded to some extent with Lydia, though they always refused to issue a coinage, being fearful, perhaps, that this would end in the establishment of a tyranny. They made beautiful pottery between 600 and 550 B.C., but after that date the wares

Fig. 22. Laconian pottery.

declined; the Spartans ceased from outside trade, and adopted a policy of rigorous economic isolation.

We cannot deal one by one with the various states of Greece during the Dark Ages; most of these were emerging from a condition governed by tribal usage, and enacting laws, though in the majority of cases we have only vague references to these, such as the abolition of the vendetta by the people of Elis, and the law of Oxylus, in the same state, forbidding the mortgaging of land for debt. In only one state have we really clear evidence, and that is Athens.

Attica had long been occupied by a population descended from the First and Second Peoples of Thessaly, perhaps Hellenized by some immigrants from Boeotia, who had used the grey Minyan ware. It seems likely that these were all peasants dwelling in humble villages, though a few of them had occupied the Acropolis at Athens, which had not yet become the capital of the country. In so far as there was a capital, or a centre for common religious worship, this was at Eleusis, where the Thessalian group practised the cult of the mother goddess that they had brought with them from Asia Minor, worshipping her under the Hellenic name of Demeter.

About 1275 B.C., as we have seen in *The Horse and the Sword*, Perseus drove out from the Peloponnese into Attica a number of Ionians, who appear to have been a mixture of Hellenes and Cretan settlers in Argolis. These, who were more civilized than the autochthones of Attica, soon became the richer and more influential class.

Before their arrival in Attica these Ionians had been organized into Genoi or Gentes, containing as a rule about thirty families in each; the genos claimed, it would appear, common descent. These Genoi had been combined in groups of thirty into Phratries, which also, but probably without reason, claimed common descent. There were twelve of these Phratries, divided in groups of three among four tribes, each again claiming common descent, though in this case the claim was certainly fictitious. Since this so-called tribal organization is found among those Ionians who had migrated to Asia Minor from the Peloponnese on the arrival of the Dorians, we must assume that it had arisen before the Ionians arrived in Attica. For some administrative purposes these 'tribes' were each divided into four Trittyes, and these again into four Naucraries.

It is claimed by some authorities that even some of the Genoi were loose aggregates of families, not derived from a common ancestor, but a considerable number of them seem to have been true clans, especially those known as Eupatrids. These Eupatrids were undoubtedly a privileged class, and for long held all the power in their own hands.

At an early date the humble villages of Attica seem to have coalesced into a number of small states; tradition says that there were twelve of these. The policy of the Ionian Eupatrids was, however, to reduce the number of these states so as to add to the importance of the survivors. A policy of coalescence, known as Synoecism, began to be carried out about 1000 B.C., and before 700 B.C. it had been completed and the whole of Attica was under the rule of Athens, though for certain religious purposes Eleusis still remained the sacred city.

The inhabitants of Attica, whether autochthones or Eupatrids, were essentially peasants, some of whom had taken to trade to augment the meagre produce of their farms, for the land was proverbially poor, so poor that, according to Thucydides, it had never attracted invaders. Some of these people were shepherds, tending their flocks, mainly of goats, upon the mountain sides, and sleeping for the most part in caves and rude shelters. They lived largely on milk and cheese, and bartered any surplus for grain. The majority, however, were peasants, cultivating a few acres of arable land and possessing small groves of olive trees. Even those living in Athens, though they may have been engaged mainly in commerce or in public life, owned their few acres of land, which they cultivated themselves with the help of their families; the modern system of landlord and tenant had not developed, and the only tenants were those who cultivated land belonging to cities or temples. All were very poor as measured by later standards, and luxury of any kind was unknown.

Tradition, probably quite correctly, related that Athens was first governed by a line of kings, though the list of these monarchs that has come down to us is clearly in great measure fictitious. Codrus, whose death at the hands of the Dorian invaders was described in *The Horse and the Sword*, is said to have been the last to bear that title, but it is added that his descendants for many generations continued to rule as Archons for life, until in the time of Cleidius, about 724 B.C., the term of office was reduced to ten years, and after the termination of the reign of Eryxius, in 683 B.C., Creon was appointed to hold office for one year only, and the post, now made annual, was thrown open to any Eupatrid. Most authorities doubt the accuracy of this account, and believe that kings in all but name survived until the institution of the annual and elective archonship in 683 B.C.

The rule of Athens thus came into the hands of Archons, annually elected by and from the Eupatrids, and before long there were ten such archons, among whom the administrative work was divided. To advise them they had a council, known as the Boulé, which met near the entrance to the Acropolis on a rocky eminence called the Areopagus or Mars' Hill. These Archons and the Boulé administered justice according to customary law, and their decisions became precedents, so that a more complete body of law arose. These, at the instructions of the Boulé, were codified by Draco in 624 B.C.

The Draconian law was considered very severe by later writers, but of this we have no means of judging, since one provision of the code which was not repealed is all that has come down to us. This divided homicide into several categories, and provided several courts to try the different types of cases. Though a serious attempt had been made by the Eupatrids to deal justly with their subjects, the code by which they worked was very drastic. The poorer peasants were ground down by the richer Eupatrids, all were heavily in debt, and many had sold their children and even themselves into slavery in an endeavour to repay their loans.

The great mass of the people, groaning under these heavy burdens, was ready for revolt, and in 612 B.C. Cylon, who had won great successes at the Olympic games, and was in consequence a popular hero, led a revolution and endeavoured to set himself up as tyrant. The revolution failed and Cylon was arraigned before the Archon, Megacles, a member of the Alcmaeonid family, by whom he was severely punished. Henceforward the Eupatrids became more unpopular than ever, and the Alcmaeonidae were singled out for special abuse and considered an accursed stock. The people felt that the whole country needed purifying, and they went to Crete for a holy man to purge their sins away. Epimenides of Knossos, who came over at the invitation of the people, was a holy man of that frenzied type that we have already noted among some of the Cretan families in Greece. He came and held gatherings, somewhat like modern revivalist meetings, and, though the people were to some extent comforted, the severe rule of the Eupatrids remained unchanged.

What the prophet failed to attain was, however, achieved almost immediately by a reforming law-giver. Solon, a Eupatrid, a member of the Neleid family that claimed descent from Poseidon and so was almost certainly of Cretan extraction, had been compelled, owing to the prodigality of his father, to become a trader, and in that capacity had visited many cities in Greece and Asia Minor. He was elected Archon in 594 B.C., and his first reforms made him so popular that he was invited to become tyrant of the city. This position he refused, but he set himself to reform the laws and most of the troubles that had beset the people soon vanished.

The most important enactments of Solon were the liberation of all slaves and the prohibition of slavery in the future, the cancellation of all debts secured on the lands or the persons of the debtor or members of his family, and finally a depreciation of the coinage by 27 per cent. These measures were adopted, though slavery was reintroduced later. This inflation and cancellation of debts solved the immediate difficulties, and the economic condition of the state improved at once. In later days the Athenians, while approving of these drastic actions under circumstances of abnormal depression, felt that they were emergency measures never to be repeated if the state was to preserve the sanctity of contracts, and it is significant that during the whole of their later history such measures were never even contemplated.

With a view to removing the abuses due to the uncontrolled exercise of authority by the Eupatrids, Solon reorganized the people of Attica on a system that almost wholly ignored status and paid attention only to wealth. While the tribes, phratries, and genoi still remained, for constitutional purposes and for taxation he divided the people into four classes according to their means.

The highest class was the Pentacosiomedimni, or possessors of land producing annually the value of 500 medimni, or about 700 bushels, of corn. This class was the most heavily taxed, but had the exclusive privilege of supplying candidates for the Archonship.

The second class was the Hippeis or knights, the annual value of whose land was equivalent to something between 300 and 500 medimni. They were less heavily taxed and had to provide themselves with horses and when required to serve the state in the cavalry.

The third class was the Zeugites, the annual value of whose land equalled from 200 to 300 medimni. These were taxed still more lightly and were liable to service in the heavy-armed infantry.

Lastly there was the fourth class, the name of which is uncertain. This contained those whose lands brought in less than the value of 200 medimni of corn, or who had no land at all. This class contained the large majority of the inhabitants of Attica; they were free from taxation and shared the privilege of electing the Archons from among the candidates put forward from their number by the Pentacosiomedimni.

Thus an organization depending upon wealth, which Aristotle termed a Timocracy, was substituted for the Aristocracy that had hitherto existed. The other laws of Solon are too many to enumerate here; he stated that they were not the best conceivable, but the best that he could expect the people to sanction, and they passed them without opposition. Then, having extracted from the inhabitants a promise not to revoke these laws for ten years, he left the city and set out on extensive travels, to Egypt, Cyprus, and Asia Minor, where he is said to have met Croesus, the last king or tyrant of Lydia, though chronological discrepancies make it difficult for us to accept the story.

Solon returned to Athens in 562 B.C. to find Attica in a turmoil between contending parties, one of which was headed by his kinsman Pisistratus. In spite of remonstrances from the law-giver the latter succeeded in 560 B.C. in making himself tyrant of the city, a position from which he was driven by his opponents, Megacles and Lycurgus. After a time these two fell out, and Megacles invited Pisistratus to return, but quarrelled with him shortly afterwards and sent him again into exile. In 550 B.C. Pisistratus returned and for the third time became tyrant of Athens, where he ruled with mildness, preserving the laws of Solon, until his death in 527 B.C.

He was succeeded in his tyranny by his sons Hippias and Hipparchus, but the latter was assassinated in 514 B.C., after which Hippias became so cruel and suspicious that the people expelled him in 510 B.C. This expulsion was carried out with the help of the Spartans, but largely owing to the activity of Clisthenes, the son of Megacles. To this statesman the city owed another reform, which made its constitution still more democratic.

It will be remembered that Solon, though he reorganized the people on a basis of wealth for purposes of government and taxation, had nevertheless left the organization of the Ionian tribes and their subdivisions untouched. Clisthenes abolished these, and set up in their place ten tribes, organized on a territorial basis, subdividing these into a number of demes or townships. These new tribes included the whole of the population, even resident aliens and emancipated slaves. The government now became popular, for, as Herodotus tells us, Clisthenes took into partnership the people who had been before excluded from almost everything.

While statesmen on the mainland were engaged in promulgating laws and framing constitutions, the leading inhabitants in some of the oversea colonies were turning their attention to other matters. We have seen that some Ionians, the Hellenized inhabitants of Cretan extraction, had left the eastern Peloponnese on the arrival of the Dorians, and had settled on or near the coast of Asia Minor. Here they had founded twelve cities, ranging from Phocaea in the north to Miletus in the south, less than ninety miles apart. These cities, most of them on the coast of Lydia, were busily engaged in commerce, from which their inhabitants obtained considerable wealth that gave some of them ample leisure to pursue their own studies. Thus it happened that several of these, especially in Miletus, turned their attention to speculations concerning the origin of things.

These studies were pursued with great vigour at Miletus, where, according to tradition, the Ionians had been preceded by a body of Cretans, expelled from Knossos by Minos. It was at Miletus that Thales, the first of the Greek philosophers, lived and taught. He is said by some to have been of Phoenician extraction, which may mean only that he was a descendant of one of the early Cretan settlers; he was born at Miletus about 640 B.C. and, though he travelled considerably and stayed for a time in Egypt, he spent most of his time in his native city, where he lived a bachelor and died at the age of 90 in 550 B.C. He was a great student of geometry and astronomy, and formu-

lated some of the statements laid down later by Euclid, and was
the first to predict a solar eclipse. He taught that all things
were ultimately derived from water and would eventually return
to that element. He had two great disciples among his fellow
colonists, Anaximander and Anaxamines. The former, who
lived from 610 to 547 B.C., was learned in astronomy and geography, introduced the sun-dial, and composed a geographical
treatise accompanied by a map engraved upon copper. Anaxamines, who flourished about 544 and was living as late as 480
B.C., varied the teaching of his master by stating that the origin
of everything was air.

These three philosophers belonged to the Ionian school, and
were followed by Heracleitus, a native of Ephesus, who was
living about 513 B.C. and held that fire was the origin of all
things, and by Anaxagoras, who was born at Clazomenae in
499 B.C., and in 480 B.C. migrated to Athens, where he lived
for thirty years. He abandoned to some extent the teachings
of his masters, and put forward the view that a supreme intelligence had imparted form and order to a pre-existing chaos.
For teaching this he was indicted for impiety by the Athenians
in 450 B.C., and to escape death he was compelled to flee to
Lampsacus, where he died at the age of 72 in 428 B.C.

Another school of philosophy was founded by Xenophanes,
a native of Colophon, who, at the age of 25, left his native city
in 546 B.C., when it was taken by the Persians, and took refuge
in Elea on the west coast of south Italy. In his philosophy,
known as the Elean, he maintained that nature and god were
one, and he denounced Homer for his description of the deities
of Olympus. His philosophy was developed by his pupil Parme-
nides, who was born at Elea about 513 B.C., and visited Athens
in 448 B.C., and later by the latter's disciple Zeno, who was born
at Elea in 488 B.C. and accompanied his master to Athens.

Besides these two schools of philosophy a third arose in the

Ionian area. The author of this was Pythagoras, who was born in Samos about 580 B.C. He was a disciple of Thales and Anaximander, then travelled extensively in the east and visited Egypt, and during his wanderings seems to have picked up a number of philosophical ideas which were already gaining currency in Asia. He was an expert in geometry and arithmetic, and seems to have been interested in the theory of numbers; he was also a believer in the transmigration of souls.

Thus there arose among the small Ionian community three systems of philosophy, from which most of the later philosophies of Greece were derived. Except for mathematics and astronomy there was little attempt to derive knowledge from the direct study of material objects, animate or inanimate, and it was sought to solve all problems by pure reason. The germs of this philosophy seem to have come from Cretan sources, though doubtless there were contributions from Egypt, where geometry had long been studied. Only in the case of Pythagoras do there seem to have been contributions from the thought of India and the regions lying to the far east, and these do not appear to have taken root or to have flourished in Greek soil.

BOOKS

Cambridge Ancient History, vol. iii (Cambridge, 1925).
GROTE, GEORGE. *History of Greece*, vol. i (London, 1846).
ZIMMERN, A. E. *The Greek Commonwealth* (Oxford, 1911).

6

The King of Kings

BETWEEN the concentrated mountain knots of the Pamir, north of western India, and of Armenia, long ranges run in sweeping, overlapping curves, enclosing great basins without outlet to the sea. This system of desert basins, framed by

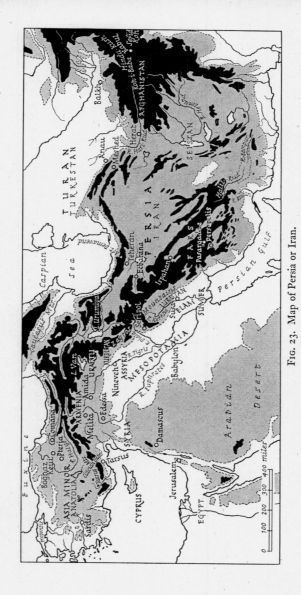

FIG. 23. Map of Persia or Iran.

mountain ranges that are more fertile in some parts, is called Iran, the land of light, in contrast with Turan, the land of darkness, the modern Turkistan, stretching away as lowland steppe desert beneath the northern edge of the mountain border of Iran.

From the south of the Pamir the high Hindu Kush stretches westwards and is replaced later by the Koh-i-baba, and between them is a high pass, communicating from Balkh on the Turan side to Kabul and so to India on the south. Farther west is the range of the Sefid-Koh with streams flowing westwards parallel to its length and feeding the Hari-Rud that cuts a gorge north-wards to lose itself in the waste. A little way from one of these westward-flowing streams stands Herat, famous like Balkh in legendary history. West of the Hari-Rud gorge a double line of lower hills stretches north-westwards, and below them on the Turanian side lies the ancient Anau, discussed in Volumes III to VI of this series, while Meshed, sacred from the early days of Islam but without as yet known earlier history, stands in the long hollow between the two lines of hills. The high range south of the Caspian rises near Teheran to 18,600 feet in the volcanic peak of Demavend. Farther west the mountains take a north-westward turn towards Armenia.

Thence stretch south-eastwards the serried ranks of the Zagros mountains with peaks sometimes above 16,000 feet in height and valleys often parallel with the mountain lines but mostly discharging westward through deep defiles. As even the valleys are usually 5,000 to 6,000 feet above sea-level the whole region is high land. Its different parts have been named differ-ently at different times, mainly because of changes of name among the groups inhabiting them. North of the Diala river the Mesopotamian side of the mountains, at any rate, may be called in a broad sense Kurdistan, and has long had a population including rather fair elements that seem to have come in ancient days from the northern steppe. South of the Diala the next section, again on the Mesopotamian side, is known as Luristan, grading southward into the ancient Elam. In the latter region, near the Kerkha river, is Susa, discussed in Chapter 4 of *Peasants and Potters*. The ancient Ecbatana lay farther north than Susa but east-south-east of the Diala. To the south of the ancient Elam the hill-lines are more arid and the valleys in many cases do not drain out to sea. Here is the region of Fars, in which lay the capitals of the Persian Empire, Pasargadae and Persepolis.

It would be unprofitable for the present purpose to continue this description of the physical features into other parts of Iran and to give an enumeration of the various basins and their framing ranges, but reference must be made to one of these basins called in antiquity Seistan, with a great lake still fed by the river Helmund from the Afghan east. It preserves memories of ancient fertility and greatness.

Whereas a great deal is now known concerning the early history of the Mesopotamian and Arabian regions, the evidences for Iran are sparse. No implements or other evidence of life of the Old Stone Age are recorded, and it may well be that in this highland area the glaciations of the Pleistocene time were very persistent. Whether epipalaeolithic or related cultures penetrated Iran, or reached Siberia and the Pacific from the west across the steppe farther north, is not yet clear, since negative evidence is unsatisfactory, at least until very detailed surveys have been made.

The melting of ice on the mountains in the relatively warm Atlantic period, called by climatologists the Atlantic phase, gave a good water-supply to Mesopotamia, but may have had less useful effects in the mountains themselves. Susa, in Elam, is one of the most ancient sites of civilization and is noted for its early multi-coloured pottery. Somewhat similar pottery is also found in the lowest layers of civilized settlement at Anau, while

Persepolis has yielded mud-walled houses that may well go back to the fourth millennium B.C. Herzfeld has found not far from Teheran pottery with black decoration on a greenish or buff background, while in the *Geographical Journal* for February 1934, Sir Aurel Stein reports his discovery in 1932 and 1933 of similar pottery from the basins of the Bampur, the Halil Rud, the Bulak, and the Rudan as well as from several other sites; it is known that the multi-coloured pottery tradition at Anau did not persist. On the whole it seems probable that a certain amount of settled life, with crops and stock, did establish itself in Iran and Turan and that it was influenced both from Mesopotamia and from the European steppe borders farther west. This seems to have been the second major movement of *Homo sapiens* and his cultures north of the great mountains of Asia, and in this connexion it is well to recall the finding of painted pottery, with resemblances to that of the steppe lands, by Andersson and Arne in northern China, as mentioned on page 141 of *The Steppe and the Sown*. Woolley suggests that early influences from the northern steppe borders affected Sumer.

At some early period, but perhaps when these rudiments of civilization had penetrated to the south of Siberia and the north of Mongolia and China, men learned to use the horse, probably a native of the snowy valleys between Mongolia and Siberia, while it is probable also that already the early peoples of the steppe farther west in Turkistan had learned to control the herds of cattle and sheep.

The Turkistan steppe was the scene of great events in the second millennium B.C., when the Indo-Aryan barbarians poured out from it towards India, armed with horse and sword, and related peoples pressed into Europe; somewhat earlier the horse reached Mesopotamia, and the power of the Mitanni had its hey-day in what is now Kurdistan. It is not known whether these outpourings were dictated by drought, or by the pressure of the yellowish brown broad-heads of the Mongolian plateau, who presumably had much to do with the early history of the horse as an adjunct of man. At any rate henceforth that type became increasingly important in central Asia and may well be what is described under the name of Turanian; it is frequently contrasted with the older Indo-Aryan long-headed, tall, and often rather fair people. These peoples have been discussed in Chapter 7 of *The Horse and the Sword*.

In Chapter 1 we have given a sketch of the successive lords of the northern steppe, especially in south Russia, during the last millennium B.C., the Cimmerians, the Scythians, and the Sarmatians. It would seem that the later steppe peoples were more affected by north central Asiatic elements than were the earlier groups. The Cimmerians and the people of Urartu or Armenia appear as opponents of the Assyrians, who were also concerned to hold back the Medes, a people of the valleys of the Zagros mountains north of Elam. It should be mentioned in passing that relief carving, said to date back to the second millennium B.C., has been found both towards Armenia, in valleys leading to Lakes Urumiya and Van, and at Seripol near the southern feeder of the Diala river, but more important, in the present state of knowledge, are the bronzes from this region, now Luristan, found by tomb-robbers in recent years.

Godard, who claims that he is the only European who has visited the site of these tombs, considers that these are the graves of Kassite chieftains and date from the centuries immediately following their expulsion from Babylonia. He argues that the earliest of these graves date from the twelfth century B.C., when bronze was giving way to iron, since a few bronze swords have been found, while iron weapons are present in larger numbers. Godard suggests that quite early the art exhibited in these bronzes received influences from an allied people, who penetrated Luristan from the north and eventually settled in Transcaucasia. This art, he thinks, reached its maturity between the ninth and the sixth centuries B.C., when it received further influences from Assyria, and it continued to the Achaemenid period, when it came suddenly to an end. Contenau, on the other hand, believes that the majority of the bronzes belong to the seventh century, and it seems to us that this is a more likely date, though it appears probable, from the presence of bronze

FIG. 24. Bronze axe from Luristan.

swords in some of the graves, that these may go back possibly as far as the ninth or even the tenth century.

The graves usually contain a horse's bone, though no complete skeletons of this animal have been found in them; the grave furniture, however, almost always contains horse's harness, especially bits. This clearly indicates that the people buried here were horsemen, who, in all probability, had come originally from the northern grasslands. We can hardly believe that it was the Kassites who were responsible for the creation or even the patronage of such a virile art, for during the long period of their reign at Babylon art was permitted to decline. It seems to us that it is to the Medes that we should ascribe these bronzes, which may well have been made by Mesopotamian craftsmen, though it would appear that some Scythic influences are present in some of the later examples.

History is quite clear as to the Medes being the predecessors of the Persians as lords in the Zagros mountains, and the Assyrian power grew up partly as a defence of the lowland against them, though doubtless it owed a good deal to the introduction of the horse, for which animal Assyria was better suited than was Babylonia.

The early history of the Persians is, as usual, legendary; Kaiomurs is supposed to have ruled over them at Balkh about 1000 B.C. This king is said to have extended his possessions, and we may imagine that he passed south into what is now Iran, since it is there that his descendants are said to have resided. In due course he was succeeded by his grandson and great-grandson, and about 850 B.C. by the latter's son Jamshyd, who is said to have been a magnificent monarch, to have introduced iron to the Persians and greatly to have improved their economic position. They say that in Persepolis were 'the courts where Jamshyd gloried and drank deep'. In his old age, however, he grew tyrannical and was driven from the throne by Zohâk, who is said to have been the son of Mardas, a king in the west, probably in Mesopotamia, and perhaps Marduk-zakir-shum, king of Babylon from 850 to 820 B.C. Zohâk was more tyrannical than the monarch he had ousted, and eventually he had to give way before the great-grandson of Jamshyd, Feridoon, who is said to have bound Zohâk with chains of iron over an abyss on Mount Demavend.

After a long and glorious reign Feridoon was succeeded in about 700 B.C. by Minoutchehr, after the death of whose son, Newder, the kingdom passed under several usurpers until it came into the hands of Kaikobád, who is said to have ruled at Persepolis, and at whose death it devolved upon his son, Kei Kaoos. This king appears to have married first of all a daughter of the king of Syria, and some years later a descendant of Feridoon, and by her to have been the father of Siawusch.

Kei Kaoos is said to have reigned at Ispahan, and it was during his reign that fierce struggles took place with Afrasiab, the king of Turan, whose capital was at Balkh. While these wars were being waged he was assisted by the hero, Rustem, the ruler of Seistan, whose tragic meeting with his son Sohrab is so well known. Though the account of these exploits has reached us only through tradition, the germ of the story is probably to some extent trustworthy, for it seems likely that in Kei Kaoos we may recognize the king known to Greek tradition as Akhaemenes, and that his son Siawusch is the same as Trispes. According to the Persian tradition Siawusch married Feringuiz, daughter of Afrasiab, and was slain by his father-in-law, after which Kei Kaoos annexed Turan and drove its king into exile.

According to the same tradition Siawusch left an only posthumous son, Kei Khosroo or Kaikhosrú, but the Greek version states that Trispes had two sons, Cyrus and Ariamnes; the latter was grandfather of Hystaspes, the father of Darius, while the former was the father of the first Cambyses and grandfather of Cyrus the Great. The kingdom of Persia at that time is said to have included the provinces of Fars and Iran, and to have extended south-westwards to the Persian Gulf and eastwards to include Seistan; it is believed, too, that it included much of what is now Afghanistan, and perhaps a small part of Russian Turkistan.

Many students are inclined to use the hypothesis that for some centuries during the earlier part of the last millennium B.C. the climate in many regions was cooler and wetter than previously, and probably a little cooler and wetter than now. Under such climatic conditions the high valleys of Fars would have been more valuable, being less burnt up in summer and better supplied with water from melting snow. The lakes in the deeper parts of the valleys now brackish might then well have shown a better balance between inflow and evaporation and, if they had been nearly or quite fresh and more numerous than at present, that would have been a considerable asset to a resident population.

However these things may be, we find that some, at least, of the Persians were after 600 B.C. under the rule of the Medes. These occupied a frontier position, and were thus opposed to the Assyrians. In the last quarter of the seventh century the Medes and Babylonians together had broken the Assyrian power and captured Nineveh, while soon afterwards the Babylonians under Nebuchadrezzar were building a wall on their north-eastern frontier as a protection against the Medes. It was Cyaxares who broke the Assyrian power and made the Medic kingdom important; his son Astyages was taken prisoner by Cyrus and the Medic power fell in 550 B.C. Medic graves are known from various sites and usually have a forecourt with two pillars leading into the sepulchral chambers; the whole is hollowed out of a rock face. It is interesting that even centuries after the fall of the Medic power, various plants, usually of pharmacological interest, were still called Medic, but our knowledge of the Medes would be small were it not for the account given by Herodotus, especially in his first book. Here he speaks of the building of the great palace at Ecbatana, with a royal city protected by a concentric series of seven walls. Each of the walls had battlements out-topping the wall beyond it, and, according to the legend, was of a particular colour. He says that the sixth wall inwards had battlements coated with silver and the last had battlements covered with gold. Within this innermost wall were the palace and treasury, and the first king Deioces, who had won his position by the careful and even-handed dispensation of justice, lived there unseen by his subjects. His grandson, Cyaxares, was defeated by the Scythians, but after twenty-eight years recovered his power and took Nineveh.

Astyages, in the story of Herodotus, is the father of the

princess Mandane, who married a Persian prince, Cambyses, and gave birth to Cyrus the Persian. Astyages dreamed that from his daughter's womb there grew up a vine that over-shadowed all Asia, and then follows the well-known story of the order to expose the child and of the circumvention of that order by a herdsman and his wife, who exposed in his place their stillborn son. The story then relates the revolt of the Persians under Cyrus against Astyages, the king of the Medes, and the utter defeat of the latter.

Though the story of the Medes as told by Herodotus is full of sheer cruelty, the statement about the administration of justice under Deioces suggests something better, and is of interest as presaging the remarkable difference between the older despotisms and that which was soon to be built up by Cyrus the Persian.

It was claimed that this king was the son of a Persian prince Cambyses, of the family of the Achaemenidae, or descendants of Achaemenes, who is said to have led the Persians into the region of Fars. These Persians included nomadic as well as irrigating groups or tribes, and seem to have acquired elements of culture from a number of sources. Their gods at first were like those of other Aryan-speaking peoples, Varuna, Mitra, Indra, and others, gods of light and the sky, opposed to demons of darkness. Fire among them was sacred. Zoroaster, discussed in Chapter 10 of *Merchant Venturers in Bronze*, seems at an early date to have inspired the Persian tribes with an ethical system, and Ahuramazda became the supreme and cosmic god of light, representing the universal principle of goodness and truth; but the other gods remained as objects of local worship.

The Persians borrowed the idea of cuneiform writing from the people of Mesopotamia, adapting it to their tradition and not taking over the actual Elamite, Babylonian, or Assyrian forms; it is usually supposed to have been developed before the

days of Cyrus, and may have belonged to the Medes, from whom
the Persians gathered a varied cultural heritage. Many Persian
inscriptions are polyglot, using the Elamite, the Babylonian,
and sometimes the Egyptian languages, also Persian, and, in
Asia Minor, Greek as well. There was little Persian art on the
large scale before the time of Cyrus, as artistic effort in those

FIG. 25. Palace of Darius at Persepolis. Restoration by F. W. von Bissing.

days was specially linked with the building of royal cities and
the Persians were under the rule of the Medes. The palace
built by Cyrus at Pasargadae, and those erected at Persepolis
by Darius and Xerxes, were built on great terraces of stone,
and rectangular forms were in fashion; the terraces were reached
by magnificent processional stairways. Much of the walls of the
terrace-edge was made of clay, as were parts of the palaces, and
this clay has disappeared, though great pillars and stone door-
ways still stand; they are built without mortar. Reliefs on the
walls followed a rather rigid convention, and owed a good deal
to Medic, Babylonian, Hittite, Armenian, Assyrian, Lydian,
Egyptian, and Greek art; the winged figure of Pasargadae suggests this in a special degree, but Assyrian art otherwise contri-

butes very little directly. Persian seals and gems are known
chiefly from outside Iran itself. The national weapons include
the bow and arrow, as well as the lance and short sword; the
Persian noble was an expert horseman.

The Persians with this tradition of horsemanship developed
a remarkable road system from Susa to Sardis to consolidate the
power won in the spread of their empire over Asia Minor. The
Royal Road, referred to by Herodotus in the early part of his
Book V, had stations and inns along the way, and he says that
by riding 150 stades a day one could go from Sardis to Susa in
ninety days. It has been suggested that, when organization had
developed farther and changes of horses were available at many
places, the journey took much less time; one estimate even
brings it down to fifteen days. The royal road went along the
foot-hills of the Zagros north-westwards to cross the Tigris at
Nineveh. Beyond this it is supposed to have passed Edessa and
Comana on its way to the Halys, or, according to some tracings,
it went by Amida and Melita. From the Halys basin at Pteria
east of that river it struck westwards and south-westwards to
Sardis. After a time a way through the Cilician gates in the
Taurus mountains north of Tarsus was utilized. The older
road, going as it does from Susa past the Halys basin to the
west, inevitably suggests the route of commerce in the last
centuries of the third millennium B.C., mentioned in Chapter 11
of *The Way of the Sea*. It ran from Sumer to Boghaz Keui,
near the later Pteria. It is thus possible that the Persians
improved and organized communications along a track of
considerable antiquity.

Cyrus the Persian is one of the greatest figures in the world's
history. His leadership seems to have been the essential factor
of the phenomenal spread of Persian power in a quarter of
a century until it covered the greater part of south-west Asia.
It is said that he did not destroy conquered towns nor did he

usually mutilate or kill conquered kings; his aim was rather to interest the conquered in the empire he was building up, and he did this partly by showing an interest in them himself. For example, it is recorded in Ezra i, *v.* 3, that he proclaimed that some one of the Hebrews was to 'go up to Jerusalem and build the house of the Lord God of Israel', and Isaiah, in chapter xliv, *v.* 28, puts into the mouth of God the following words concerning him: 'He is my shepherd and shall perform all my pleasure; even saying to Jerusalem, Thou shalt be built.' A foreign ruler who could inspire such sentiments, and who had brave and hardy soldiers, could easily overturn decadent military powers based on crude domination. In the story of Herodotus we see something of Cyrus' contempt for those whose lives centred in the market-place. He seems to have founded a system which governed, to some extent at least, with the interests of his subjects as one of its chief concerns. The system of justice required that the services of an offender should be set against his offence, and that even a slave must not be too heavily punished for a single misdeed. The famous summary of Persian education, given by Herodotus, was that it was a training to ride, to draw the bow, and to speak the truth. The horsemen attacked and also protected the armourless archers, and on the efficiency of the cavalry everything depended.

As in the case of other heroes, legends gathered round the birth of Cyrus, and some surmise that they took the form of his conception in a Medic princess's womb through the power of a deity. The nurse who suckled him was originally a bitch, and the dog was a sacred animal in Persia. In other words there were here resemblances to the stories told of the birth of Jesus, the Buddha, Mahavira, Lao Tzu, Perseus, Moses, Sargon, and Romulus and Remus.

There was more than the idea of toleration and justice behind this great personality. He came at a time after efforts by

Ikhnaton and the beautiful Nefertiti, and later on by the magnificent Semiramis, to rise above localism to universalism in religion had failed. The Buddha was just about to appear in India, and Lao Tzu and Confucius were nearly contemporaries in China; Isaiah was prophesying in Judah, and the day of the philosophers had dawned in Greece. The Persian god, Ahuramazda, became the universal god and one seems to hear the thinkers around Cyrus saying that, whatever local names may be used, they refer to the same god, who desires justice and truth. It would be interesting, were there space, to follow the influence of all this on the development of Hebrew religion from the worship of a savage god, delighting in cruelty and bloodshed, to the later concept of Jahweh so remarkably given by Zechariah in his descriptions of the future and ideal Jerusalem.

It is probable that this remarkable development of thought was not a little aided by the fact that much of the equipment and art of the Persians was borrowed from their neighbours. The mention of road systems is a reminder that isolation was breaking down; iron had become an important item and must be bought if it could not be produced at home, and horses made it possible to carry light loads over long distances. The details given in chapter xxvii of Ezekiel's prophecy picture a state of things unthinkable a few centuries before.

BOOKS

Cambridge Ancient History, vol. iv (Cambridge, 1926).
HERODOTUS. *Histories*.
HALL, H. R. *Ancient History of the Near East* (London, 1913).

7

India of the Philosophers

IN Chapter 11 of *The Horse and the Sword* reference was made to the conquest of northern India about 1500 B.C. by people of Indo-European speech in a state of vigorous barbarism. Since the publication of that volume of *The Corridors of Time*, an important contribution to the study of Indian peoples has been published by Dr. J. H. Hutton in *The Census of India, 1931*, vol. i, part 1. In the matter of language he draws attention to the widely scattered distribution of remnants of Austro-Asiatic languages in India, though the south of India was unfortunately not surveyed linguistically, and beyond it as far as Madagascar, New Zealand, and Easter Island. This is rightly held to be evidence of their age, and suggestions have recently been made to the effect that these languages are related to the Finno-Ugrian group as well. The Austro-Asiatic group includes the Munda family, which is Indian, and the Mon-Khmer family, which seems to owe its occurrence in some parts of India to a spread from Indonesia and south-east Asia. There may well have been many comings and goings in south-east Asia in early times. Some of these languages are affected by Aryan influence.

The Dravidian group of languages, the chief varieties of which in India are Tamil, Telugu, and Kanarese, occur as far north as the Ganges in Bihar; they are also found in large patches in the Central Provinces and Orissa, and are practically universal in south India. It is believed by Rapson and others that the Dravidian languages were in widespread use in north India when the Indo-Aryan languages came in, and this makes it impossible to accept Przyluski's view that the Austro-Asiatic group pressed the Dravidian out of the north. The Dravidian languages are the younger group. Langdon thinks there are indications of Sumerian affinities of signs used by the people of the Indus civilization of the third millennium B.C. discovered by Marshall, and Hutton accepts as a provisional hypothesis the view that a language of the Indus civilization was related to the Dravidian group. Brahui, a member of this group, still survives in Baluchistan and the influence of Dravidian in north Indian Aryan languages is said to be noteworthy. Sir Aurel Stein in the *Geographical Journal* for February 1934 gives indications of numerous sites occupied by people with a culture related to that of early Mesopotamia of about 3000 B.C. in southern Persia.

Schoener has traced Dravidian-like place-names in Mesopotamia and Iran, but his views are disputed. G. W. Brown in 1930 found Dravidian affinities in the Kharrian language of the Mitanni, spoken both before and after Aryan-speaking invaders had conquered the northern part of the lowland basin of the Euphrates; these occur also in some surviving languages of the Caucasus. This all goes to support the views concerning Dravidian culture put forward by Slater some years before the ancient civilization of the Indus had been discovered, namely that that culture had relations, in part at least by land, with Mesopotamia. In detail, however, there are many contrasts between early Mesopotamia and early Indian civilization.

Hutton, following Grierson, draws attention to the existence of an inner and an outer zone of Aryan languages. The outer zone includes the North-west Frontier and western Kashmir on the one hand, and the north-west of the Deccan, a part of the Central Provinces, Bihar and Orissa, and those parts of Bengal and Assam where the old Austro-Asiatic languages do not still dominate. He proposes the hypothesis that, as this is also the main zone in India of brachycephals who may be called Alpine-Pamirian in type, there was an invasion of these people some time before that of the Indo-Aryan longheads arrived about 1500 B.C. These latter conquered and imposed their languages on most of the Punjab, Rajputana, parts of central India, and

Fig. 26. Munda and Mon-Khmer Languages.

Fig. 27. Tibeto-Chinese Languages.

Fig. 28. Dravidian Languages.

Fig. 29. Indo-Aryan Languages.

the United Provinces, and, later, on Gujarat and Nepal. It was
the language of this inner zone which evolved a script, and, as
long ago as 1867, E. Thomas argued that the Sanskrit alphabet
had its source in some scheme of writing of the inhabitants who
were established in India before these warriors arrived. The
Aryan-speaking groups seem to have borrowed alphabets where-
ever they went, as he pointed out, and now there are indications,
hardly yet fully established, that the signs on the seals of the
Indus civilization have links with the alphabets in which the
Aryan languages of India came to be written. It is an attractive
doctrine that two main Aryan-speaking waves of invasion or
immigration, an earlier broad-headed and a later very long-
headed group, spread into a country in which Dravidian languages were widely used, while Austro-Asiatic languages lingered
here and there. Rapson is inclined to think of the outer zone
of Aryan languages as a zone of extension of the Aryan area, into
which the languages penetrated with modifications as they went;
this view does not altogether contradict that of Hutton.

Hutton expands his well-known view that the first occupants
of India were Negritos, traces of whom survive in south India
and Assam. Some of the elements of phallic cults may belong
even to this stratum. A Proto-Australoid, often with an extremely long head, broad nose, and prognathous jaw, is the next
element, but it would be dangerous at present to identify these
with the original Munda-speaking elements; arguments from
the survivors in some parts are, however, suggestive. There
followed a 'Brown Race' element, to use Elliot Smith's useful
term for the moderately long-headed brunette elements of the
Mediterranean area, south-west Asia and south India, and this,
probably with brachycephalic elements also, may be linked provisionally with the Indus civilization and possibly with the
spread of the Dravidian languages. To it, or to the Proto-
Australoid element, or to both, may be ascribed some aspects

of the phallic cult, of megalith building, and of the idea of a
life-essence or soul-matter. That there followed in due course
Mesopotamian and eastern Mediterranean religious ideas, more
or less altered, seems highly probable. Marshall has shown that
the religion of the Indus civilization included a cult of the bull
and of the snake, which were also important elements in Cretan
religion, and a figure has been found which is held to be identi-
fiable with the Shiva of later Hinduism.

The old view, which has been combated in most of the
volumes of this series, was that the Aryan-speaking invaders of
1500 B.C. entered an India inhabited by lowly peoples only, and
brought civilization with them. This view was attacked by one
of us before Marshall's discoveries were made, and has not been
held by Hutton and other modern investigators. Marshall's
work has made much more probable the suggestions of E. Thomas
and others referred to above that the later civilization of India
has a large heritage from the early inhabitants. The gods of the
conquerors of 1500 B.C. were Indra, Mitra, Agni, Dyaus,
Prithivi, Varuna, as the sacred books, notably the Rig-Veda,
inform us. These all become quite subordinate in later Hinduism; they have been absorbed into the complex Hindu system
which, according to Hutton and E. J. Thomas and others, took
form especially in the region north of the Ganges, between the
Jumna and the Gogra. The view is that the Punjab was completely dominated by these invaders and as they reached the
Ganges fusion and assimilation became inevitable. They were
a warrior group, the Kshatriya, which, in course of time, and
following the development of territorial links of its members as
nobles gathering tribute from cultivators, became the Rajput
clans. In early days they hunted, raced, ate flesh in quantities,
and sacrificed animals, all features associated with the life of the
steppe-horsemen who sent out Aryan-speaking conquerors in
many directions. In Indian records dating from after the

conquest is found the statement that, while cattle may appro-
priately be sacrificed to Varuna or Mitra, it is not advisable to
offer them because this annoys the common people. This makes
Hindu reverence for cattle almost certainly a pre-conquest

FIG. 30. Figure of Brahmani bull
from Mohenjo-daro.

Indian characteristic as was suggested in *The Horse and the Sword*;
and the worship of the bull was a
feature of the Indus civilization.
Reverence for cattle is the great
feature of the Brahman caste,
which would thus have developed
from the pre-conquest life of the
country, and there are many indications of conflict between
Brahman and Kshatriya from
early times onwards, as would be
expected. Whether the Brahman caste is to be linked more with
the Aryan-speaking peoples of the outer zone or with the still
older elements of Indian life or with both need not be discussed
here; its ideas and customs no doubt owe something to all these
sources and, especially as regards marriage, also to the ideas
which spread with the Kshatriya conquest.

Chanda has well argued that Vishnu, Shiva, and Sakti are
gods of non-Aryan origin, even if Vishnu is perhaps later than the
Aryan-speaking conquerors. It seems clear that the conquerors
of 1500 B.C. found in India an established religion with a ritual
related to the life of the cattle-keeping cultivators, and impreg-
nated with very old ideas of life-essence or soul-substance, and
of ancestor worship so far as its leaders or kings were concerned.
That this religious scheme was controlled by priests who managed to maintain their prestige in face of barbarian conquerors
is highly probable, and we have here the analogy of the Christian
priesthood in post-Roman Europe facing the barbarian con-

querors and converting them into champions of the church, albeit with many feuds and excommunications. In later Hinduism Shiva, Vishnu, and Kali are far more important than Indra and the other gods of the Kshatriya. The former have doubtless absorbed into themselves elements of belief and ritual from all sorts of early stages of the development of Indian life; the bull Nandi, for example, is the vehicle of Shiva. The latter, having been the gods of a military aristocracy, do survive, but have decreased in importance because their rites are not related to local agricultural routine, and the local life has surged up again under Brahman leadership. It is thought, however, that, of the Hindu gods, Vishnu is a post-conquest development deriving from the increase of ascendancy of the male over the older female aspect in the concept of divinity.

One can picture rough conquerors spreading in India among the cultivators, finding themselves in small groups among large populations that, for the most part, could be distinguished from themselves at a glance. Restrictions on intermarriage would be emphasized to protect the small group from total immersion in the great mass; and caste, with increasing prestige of the Brahman, would develop, while links between the Brahman and the noble would multiply. Advance into the Ganges valley led to the foundation of kingdoms. Trade and commerce, both by sea and by land, began to flourish, and in the eighth century B.C. the art of writing spread through this area.

During the seventh century these petty kingdoms began to coalesce into larger units, and there arose the kingdom of Kosala, corresponding to the later kingdom of Oudh; this so increased in size that before the close of the century it had become the most important state in the northern part of Hindustan. It was some time in the sixth century that one of these petty kingdoms, that of Magadha, became prominent among its neighbours under the Sais'unaga dynasty. Bimbisara, the first king about whom we have any certain knowledge, reigned from 519 to 491 B.C.

In Chapter 11 of *The Horse and the Sword* we described the books of the Rig-Veda, the earliest sacred books of the Aryans. In the last of these, composed, it is believed, about 1000 B.C., the latest hymns seem to display an element of dissatisfaction with the worship of a multitude of gods. During the next few centuries were written a series of books in prose, known as the Brahmanas. These indicate the growth of priestly power, which is conspicuous by its absence from all but the very latest hymns of the Rig-Veda. According to the Brahmanas, 'The gods talk only to the higher castes', and the priests or Brahmans are to be treated as 'human gods'. Throughout these books there is an increasing search for unity behind the diversity of deities, and in the end was evolved a principle, known as Brahman, considered as the final reality of the universe, and this was identified with Atman, the world-soul.

Here and there in the Brahmanas are occasional references to the doctrine of rebirth, but this was developed in the seventh, or possibly in the sixth, century into the completed doctrine of the transmigration of souls, which is elaborated in the Upanishads, that were written about this time. While the Brahmanas show us a marked increase in priestly influence, the Upanishads, which attracted the attention of the Kshatriya as much as of the Brahman caste, were concerned with the development of a monistic philosophy and a high ethical teaching, involving the doctrine of rewards and punishments.

Recent studies of Jainism by Shah suggest that one of the earliest teachers of general ideas in India was Parsva, very tentatively dated to the eighth century B.C.; he taught in north India, and is known chiefly through references in Jain literature. Apparently he belonged to Benares, and emphasized the need for vows against killing, stealing, lying, and the following of illusory objects. This, however, is merely an attempt to give a short introductory statement on a subject that is still wrapped in mystery. Its interest and value lie in the suggestion that it gives of an uprise of thought critical of the formalism of immemorial ritual and, what is more important, reaching out towards ethical ideas of universal applicability. The analogy with Hebrew thought will strike every mind. In India the struggle was one against the privileged Brahmans, by now becoming a caste; and apparently it was aided at various times by princes, that is probably Kshatriya. Its efforts for ethical principles are more important than its critical activities, and the consideration of these brings us to the great teachers of the sixth century in India.

According to the Jains, they have existed as a religious group since the days of Parsva; there can at any rate be no doubt that this movement underwent a reformation under Mahavira, more or less contemporary with the great figure of Gautama, the Buddha. Followers both of Mahavira and of the Buddha accepted some of the contemporary religious ideas in India, notably that of the transmigration of souls. Caste, under these schemes, became a punishment or reward for conduct in a previous life; the goal was liberation from all bodily forms and activities, the state known as Nirvana. Both Mahavira and the Buddha are associated with the Kshatriya group, and it was not considered that their religious ideas necessarily constituted a break with the traditional religion.

Mahavira's father is said to have been a village chieftain; Siddartha, his mother, was a princess, related to Bimbisara, one of the kings who built up the early historic power of Magadha. After having attained the age of 30, Mahavira wandered about for twelve years as an ascetic, vowed to continuous chastity and the subjugation of the senses. At the end of this period he is said to have attained to complete knowledge, and the rest of his life was devoted to religious teaching. He attained Nirvana thirty years later in Pavapuri, about seven miles south-east of the town of Bihar. Some Jain scholars think that the date was

527 B.C., but 467 B.C. is claimed with rather more authority. Much in the same way there is some difference of opinion as to whether the death of the Buddha took place in 543 B.C. or in 477 B.C.; the latter date is the more probable.

The Jain view of the universe gave no place to a god, but emphasized the eternity of existence, and the cultivation of supreme intelligence as a means of liberation. It looked, in other words, towards a monistic philosophy, emphasizing the spiritual or psychical aspect. But it had a dualistic idea, as it were, on the way thither. The soul of Jiva, until it attains Nirvana, is always in combination with Ajiva, and their union creates a kind of energy, Karma, which may be interpreted as deeds of the soul, good or bad; and these influence birth and rebirth.

FIG. 31. Figure of Buddha from Gandhara, N.W. India (after 100 A.D.). The base shows Buddha with a man and a woman on either side. The throne is supported on two lions. Conventional lotus is used in the decoration.

Mention has been made of the Jains before turning to the figure of Gautama the Buddha, because the Jain movement, looking back centuries beyond the Buddha's time, gives some idea of the mental atmosphere in which the Buddha came to work. He was the son of a king of the Sakyas, living near the Himalaya, and he left home at the age of 29 seeking enlightenment, which came to him six years later under the Bo Tree at

Gaya in Magadha. After this he spent forty-five years in preaching his doctrine and then he attained Nirvana. Both concerning his birth and concerning that of Mahavira there are told miraculous stories. The authority for the life and teaching of the Buddha has long been derived from a canon, written in Ceylon in the Pali language, and dating from about the first century A.D., for Buddhism had been brought to that island by missionaries in the third century B.C. There is less ready acceptance of the authority of this canon at the present time than was formerly the case. Buddha saw the weaknesses of both sensuality and asceticism, and he sought the middle way, which was the attainment of the knowledge of truth concerning pain and its cessation through the abandonment of craving, and the attainment of the knowledge of the noble eightfold path towards this end—right thoughts, right intentions, right speech, right action, right livelihood, right effort, right mindfulness, and right concentration. Apparently the Buddha was agnostic as regards the creation of the universe and the continued existence of those who attain Nirvana. The Buddha founded an order of monks and of nuns, and sought to encourage the mind to become concentrated in mystical meditation. This was a feature of Hinduism as well. One must realize that while both Mahavira and the Buddha attracted chiefly the Kshatriya, by now beyond the stage of mere conquest in northern India, they functioned both as influences in the continuous evolution of Hindu religious tradition and as founders of largely new movements.

From the popular point of view Buddhist and Jain ideas lacked the attraction of a religion satisfied with a performance of ritual and allowing man to live under the guidance of custom. They preached the need for thought and thus sealed their fate as large-scale and durable mass movements. Schisms occurred among both Buddhists and Jains, and Buddhism passed away from the land of its birth, surviving in a very modified form with elaborate rituals in central and in south-eastern Asia. It was in fact submerged by the resurgence of the Brahman influence against Kshatriya power. Jainism has survived as the religion of a superior minority in parts of northern and north-western India. Its followers are said to be especially the wealthy people, such as money-lenders and merchants.

What has been said about the Jain and Buddhist traditions brings out for India what was a general feature among the higher civilizations of the last millennium B.C. This was the rise of abstract thought which is illustrated in the progress of Zoroastrian doctrine, in the work of the prophets of Israel, in the China of Lao Tzu and Confucius, and among the philosophers of Greece, while it was clearly foreshadowed much earlier in the development of Egyptian religion under Ikhnaton, as sketched on page 153 of *Merchant Venturers in Bronze*. Far and wide the old irrational rituals with their gods of fancy were becoming unsatisfying and men's thoughts were turning to problems of life and the universe.

While this religious development was going on in northern India, the Kshatriya were for the most part continuing their internecine struggles and also sending adventurous conquerors southwards into the Deccan. Risley argued for a Scythian invasion into north-western India about this time, but it is not generally held that this occurred. In the north, Magadha and Kosala had the usual quarrels and difficulties concerning succession. In 491 B.C. Bimbisara was slain by his son Ajatasatru, and this tragedy led to a serious war with the kingdom of Kosala. Nevertheless Magadha remained the chief power in northern India until the descendants of Bimbisara were driven out in 361 B.C. by Nanda, whose family were dispossessed of the kingdom in 321 B.C. by Chandragupta Maurya, the first Chakravarti Raja or universal monarch of India.

It was during the reign of Chandragupta that in 327 B.C.

Alexander the Great invaded India, though he failed to make a permanent conquest. Later on his general, Seleucus, king of Syria, made another but scarcely more successful attempt. India was again unified by Chandragupta's grandson, Asoka, who reigned from 266 to 227 B.C. over the whole land from the Hindu Kush and the Himalaya mountains south-westward to the region of Madras and Mysore. He was a convert to the teachings of the Buddha, and encouraged this religion throughout his dominions, besides sending missionaries to lands beyond, including the island of Ceylon.

BOOKS

The Cambridge History of India, vol. i (Cambridge, 1922).
SMITH, VINCENT A. *Early History of India* (Oxford, 1914).
HUTTON, J. H. *The Census of India, 1931*, vol. i, pt. i (Delhi, 1933).
THOMAS, E. J. *History of Buddhist Thought* (London, 1933).
SHAH, C. J. *Jainism in North India* (London, 1932).

8

Chinese Sages

TOWARDS the end of Chapter 10 of *Merchant Venturers in Bronze* we made brief mention of the fate of the last emperor of the Shang dynasty in China and the foundation of the Chou dynasty in 1122 B.C., and in Chapter 11 of *The Horse and the Sword* we gave a short account of the events that took place during the first few reigns of that dynasty. China at this time consisted of little more than the basin of the Hoang-ho and its tributary the Wei, and this area was divided up into a number of distinct kingdoms and principalities, all of which were to some extent feudatory to the early emperors of the Chou dynasty. The overlordship seems to have been fully effective until the accession of Chao-wang, the fourth monarch, in 1052 B.C., but during the fifty years of his reign the authority of the central power was weakened owing to his ineffective rule, and this weakness increased during the time of I-wang, who reigned between 934 and 910 B.C. Matters were no better under his successor, Hiau-wang, who ruled until 895 B.C., and this emperor made a horse-dealer, Fei-tze, prince of the state of Ch'in in the Wei valley, thus founding a powerful dynasty that was ultimately to supplant his successors. During the reign of Li-wang, who ascended the throne in 878 B.C., what had been the Chinese Empire became a loose confederacy of independent states, and the misdeeds of this monarch led to a rebellion in 842 B.C., when Li-wang was banished and the rule over the Chou state was handed over to the dukes of Chou and Shao. The western states became threatening during the next century, so that P'ing-wang, who reigned from 770 to 720 B.C., moved his capital eastward to Lo-yang, the modern Ho-nan-fu. The condition of the Chou state improved under the rule of Chuan-wang between 696 and 682 B.C., for that monarch established a state monopoly in iron and salt, which brought in a considerable revenue, though he remained emperor only in name.

There is some difference of opinion as to the nature of the religious ideas of the Chinese people at this time. Waley has recently expressed the view that until the early years of the fourth century B.C. religion meant nothing to the Chinese but a series of rituals to be performed, and sacrifices to be offered, to ensure the success of agriculture and lest calamity should befall the community, while moral codes and ethical ideas formed no part of this religion. Dr. H. A. Giles, on the other hand, contended that a certain sense of right-doing accompanied the worship of *Tien* or *Shang-ti,* the ruler of the universe, and has cited a number of sayings, reported to have been uttered by various early emperors, and to be found in the *Shu-king.* Furthermore, if it be contended that these speeches had been written in later times and attributed to these monarchs, many of the odes in the *Shi-king*, which were collected in the sixth century but may go back in some cases to the twelfth, contain a number of moral precepts and describe the deity as rewarding the good and punishing the bad. It is at any rate doubtful whether the Chinese people pondered much on the question of ethics until the sixth century B.C., when there appeared among them two philosophers, very different in their outlook, though both were concerned in expounding the principles of proper behaviour.

The more famous of these two philosophers was Kʻung Fu-tzu, better known to western readers as Confucius. It is said that he was born in 551 B.C. somewhere in the state of Lu in the modern province of Shantung, and that his father, Shuh-leang Heio, an officer in the army, was seventy years of age when he married Yan-Ching-tsai, the sage's mother. When about twenty years of age Confucius accepted the office of keeper of the stores of grain, and during the next year he was promoted to be the guardian of the public fields and lands. In the following year he gave up this office and devoted his time to instructing a chosen band of disciples and admirers.

While he had the greatest respect for the customs of antiquity and for ritual and sacrifice, Confucius was to some extent an agnostic. It is true that a few sayings attributed to him indicate a belief in the existence of *Tien* or *Shang-ti*, but he felt that mankind knew little of the major deities, while as to the lesser gods his view may be summed up in his famous saying, 'Respect the spirits, but keep them at a distance'. His teaching, therefore, was concerned not with dogma but with right behaviour, and the constant theme of his remarks was what the superior man should do under a variety of circumstances. Though he countenanced the ceremonies for driving out evil spirits performed by the villagers, he was on the whole averse from superstitious practices, and his appeal was mainly to the educated classes; he is reported to have said, 'I do not open the truth to one who is not eager after knowledge, nor do I help any one who is not anxious to explain himself. When I have presented one corner of a subject, and the listener cannot from it learn the other three, I do not repeat my lesson.'

Though various works, mainly of an historical character, are said to have been written or edited by Confucius, our chief knowledge of his teaching is derived from the writings of Mong-tzu, better known as Mencius, but there are some who believe that this later sage, who lived between 372 and 289 B.C., was responsible for the thoughts and maxims to which he gave utterance, and that he attributed these to Confucius, whose name was already much revered, that they might receive greater attention from the people. It is probable, however, that, if the sayings quoted by Mencius were not actually uttered by the earlier sage, they were at least in keeping with his teaching.

A more shadowy person is the other great sage, known in his lifetime as Lao Tan but to posterity as Lao Tzu. In later days it was said that he was born in 604 B.C., and became keeper of the archives for the state of Chou. It is related that about 498 B.C., when the sage was already 106 years of age, he received a visit from Confucius, who was anxious to consult the state papers. It is said that they had a long discussion, when the elder sage rebuked the younger for his preoccupation with worldly affairs. Soon after this Lao Tzu retired from his post and went to live quietly in the country, but as the state of Chou fell into disorder he passed into Honan and thence westward into the mountains where he disappeared. There are no contemporary references to him, and the first occasion on which he was mentioned was in the late fourth or early third century, when the philosopher Chuang Tzu attributed to him many of the ideas that he was advancing. Some think that the real Lao Tzu was a treasurer of the Chou state about 374 B.C., whose name also was Lao Tan.

It was about 500 B.C. that iron swords replaced those of bronze, though the newer metal seems to have been used already for some time for ploughshares and for other agricultural implements. It was about this time, too, that the various Chinese states began quarrelling with one another, the stronger swallowing up the weaker, until only a few were left. This period of about 250 years has been called by the Chinese historians the period of the contending states. The kings of Chou were more and more losing their influence, and were emperors only in name, while the Ch'in state was growing at the expense of its neighbours. At length the Ch'in waged direct war against the Chou, and after a long period of strife Shi Hwang-ti, the lord of the Ch'in, finally deposed the last of the Chou kings, and became the first undoubted emperor of all the Chinese states.

It was during this period of contention that the thinking portion of the Chinese people became disillusioned, and sought after something better. The conquering Ch'in followed the philosophy known as realist or legalist, which was attributed to Shang, a statesman living in that country in the fourth century B.C. This philosophy was one of rank selfishness, teaching that each should acquire what he could, that the strong and ruthless would flourish and the weak would be subject to them. This philosophy was in keeping with the barbaric condition of the people in Ch'in, mostly living in a pastoral condition and much mixed with Tartar blood.

As a contrast to this there arose among the agricultural people the doctrine of quietism, preaching love to one's neighbour and gentle behaviour to all. This seems to have arisen out of the ritual preparation of the sacrificer for the reception of the descending spirit, which developed into a cleansing of the heart to be a fit home for the soul. This led to contemplation, to *Tso-wang*, a sitting with a blank mind, to Yoga, and to the Zen philosophy. Based on this quietism arose the sect of *Mo Tzu*, which demanded that its adherents should 'feel towards all people under heaven exactly as one feels towards one's own people, and regard other states exactly as one regards one's own state'. This sect, which seems to have arisen in the Shantung peninsula, considered that its teaching was derived from Confucius.

By degrees quietism took two diverse forms, one based on the supposed teachings of Confucius, and preached early in the fourth century by Mencius, the other advocated, amongst others, by Chuang Tzu towards the close of the same century, and attributed to the shadowy Lao Tzu. The Confucians addressed themselves mainly to the educated classes and were concerned with the right behaviour of rulers and the attitude towards them to be adopted by the ruled. They based their tenets on what was supposed to have been the teaching and practice of the early emperors, and hoped in time to develop an ideal state, where every one would fall into his proper place, according to his intelligence and the amount of his education, under a model ruler or beneficent despot.

The other school thought little of the world and were concerned only with personal behaviour. They preached a form of relativity, that nothing was either long or short, as well as the practice of inactivity and of leaving things to follow their own courses without interference. Their teaching might be summed up in the phrase *solvitur ambulando*, or in a more homely way by the nursery rhyme of Little Bo-peep:

> *Leave them alone and they'll come home,*
> *Bringing their tails behind them.*

Thus this form of quietism grew, especially among the humbler and less educated classes, and about 240 B.C. its philosophy was summed up in a work entitled *Tao Tê Ching*, 'The Way and its Power', dedicated and ultimately ascribed to Lao Tzu. This work became the authoritative scripture of the sect that from its title took the name of Taoism.

To return to Shi Hwang-ti, he was nominally the fourth king of the Ch'in dynasty, but in reality the first to reign undisputed over the whole of the territory of Chou. On his accession he realized the impossibility of progress so long as the Chinese were distributed among a number of states, loosely federated and more often than not at war among themselves, and usually paying only nominal fealty to an emperor. He wished to be an emperor in fact as well as in name, and to bring under his rule the whole of the black-haired race, as the Chinese called themselves. This ambition met with strenuous opposition from the educated classes, steeped in the history and traditions of their country, and, under the influence of Confucian teaching, very averse from any radical change in the constitution. Against every proposal of his, these *literati* cited deeds and sayings of the emperors of old as unanswerable arguments, until in desperation he decided on a momentous step, nothing less than to destroy all the written works in the country, except those relating to divination and medicine. Thus occurred the famous 'fire of the Ch'in'. In spite of the determined resistance of the learned, many of whom elected to be executed rather than permit their cherished volumes to be committed to the flames, he had this decree carried out with the utmost ruthlessness.

After that, Shi Hwang-ti proclaimed himself emperor over the whole Chinese people, and started to provide better material conditions in the country. With a view to improving the communications between the various states, he caused roads to be constructed and bridges to be built across the rivers, and encouraged every form of rapid transport that was available at that time. Since the Tartar tribes from the northern steppe were making constant inroads into the settled country, he erected the Great Wall, stretching from the mountains to the sea, to keep these marauders at bay, and under his rule a measure of prosperity returned to the black-haired people.

During this time the art of the country became freed from

Fig. 32. Han glazed pottery. Models of buildings and animals.

the formalism that had hitherto characterized its products, and tended to depict animals in motion rather than conventional figures at rest. In this it was much influenced by the Scythic art, that had for a few centuries past been in vogue throughout most parts of Asia and eastern Europe as well.

After the death of Shi Hwang-ti in 210 B.C. his successors were unable to carry on his virile rule, and the country again fell into disorder. From this it was saved by a man from the Han state, who overthrew the last feeble monarch of the Ch'in dynasty, and in 206 B.C. set himself up as Kaoti, first emperor of the Han dynasty. His revolt was supported by the educated classes, the Confucians, and those quietists who followed the teachings attributed to Lao Tzu. In return for this support he inaugurated a search for such written works as had survived, which appeared in some numbers from the recesses of caves, the roofs of houses, and the banks of rivers, while many ancient texts were taken down from the lips of old men, whose retentive memories had preserved much that would otherwise have been lost. With the Han dynasty China entered upon its truly historic period.

BOOKS

Douglas, R. K. *Confucianism and Taoism* (London, 1889).
Giles, H. A. *Religions of Ancient China* (London, 1905).
Giles, H. A. *Confucianism and its rivals* (London, 1915).
Hirth, F. *The Ancient History of China* (New York, 1908).
Waley, A. *The Way and its Power* (London, 1934).

9

The Birth of Rome

IT will be remembered that in Chapter 3 of *Merchant Venturers in Bronze* we described the arrival in the Po valley of a new people, who burned their dead, and lived in villages, surrounded by artificial streams, near the banks of the rivers. These settlements are called *terremare* and the objects found in them suggest that they were first made some time in the Early Bronze Age and abandoned about 1200 B.C. MacIver has suggested that invaders continued to arrive for about 150 years, though the oldest known settlements of these new-comers cannot be dated

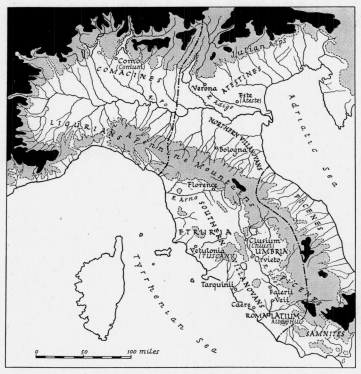

FIG. 33. Map of Central Italy showing areas of cremation and inhumation.

earlier than about 1050 B.C. The civilization of these new people is known as the Villanova culture, from the site on the outskirts of Bologna where it was first found; there are, however, at least four types of this culture, used apparently by four different but allied groups of invaders, to whom MacIver has given distinctive names, based in some cases on the Latin names of certain cities, around which these remains have been discovered.

Inhumation was in the Neolithic Age general throughout Italy, yet through part of the Bronze Age and during the Early Iron Age cremation was the rule in a broad belt from the head of the Adriatic Sea to the Etruscan coast of the Tyrrhenian Sea. MacIver says its boundary ran on the east from just north of Rimini to the Alban Hills east of Rome, and on the west from a point west of Verona to another just north of the mouth of the Arno. We attempt to define this area more exactly in Fig. 33. To the west of this belt were numerous indigenous tribes of uncertain origin, who may for convenience be aggregated under the name of Ligurians, the people occupying most of this territory a few centuries later. East of the belt lived several tribes, the best known of which were the Samnites, to all of which MacIver has allotted the name of Picenes, from the Piceni, who formed the most important member of the group when the Romans first came into contact with them. Beyond the Picene group there were other tribes in Apulia, called for convenience Apulians, while the Siculi, who gave their name to Sicily, were occupying the greater part of Calabria.

The four cremating Villanova groups of MacIver are firstly the Northern Villanovans, occupying the country around Bologna, between the Adige and the Apennines, secondly the Southern Villanovans, living in Tuscany and the adjoining parts of Umbria and Latium, thirdly the Atestines, whose remains have been found chiefly around Este, the ancient Ateste, and who occupied most of the country between the Adige and the Julian Alps, and lastly the Comacines, the evidence for whose existence comes mainly from the regions lying to the south of the lakes, around Como, the ancient Comum. Some of these, almost certainly the Southern Villanovans, were known in the fifth century as Umbrians, or Ombricoi as Herodotus calls them.

MacIver has suggested that these tribes had come round the head of the Adriatic Sea from the north of the Balkan peninsula, but the close relationship between the Villanova culture and that of Hallstatt, to be described in Chapter 10, suggests that some, at least, had migrated from the eastern end of the Alps. Their custom of burying the urns containing the ashes of the dead close together in small cemeteries seems to connect them, if only remotely, with the urn-field people of the Lausitz culture, while the presence of the horse, attested by bits and other items of harness, found among their earliest remains, suggests that among their leaders were herdsmen, probably from the slopes of the eastern Alps. The nature of the country, as well as the archaeological remains that have come to light, makes it probable that the Northern Villanovans consisted mainly of the urn-field people, while the mountain region of the Apennines, Tuscany, and Latium would have proved more attractive to the pastoral folk.

Soon after the arrival in Italy of these new Villanovan tribes, iron seems to have become known throughout the peninsula, and it had reached the Northern Villanovans at any rate as early as 1050 B.C., though it was not yet plentiful. Some have thought that the new metal, like the new people, had arrived from the eastern Alps, but the dates are against this, since it is difficult to prove the presence of iron in that quarter before 900 B.C. Moreover, as MacIver has shown, there is clear evidence that the knowledge of iron spread through Italy from the south-east, and fine iron swords, dating from a very early time, have been found in Calabria, where the industry remained in advance of that found farther north.

Around the southern coasts of Italy are a number of places whose names end in -*ntum*: Sipuntum, reputed to have been founded by Diomedes, a Danaan king of Argolis; Hydruntum, said to be a most ancient town; Tarentum, thought to be of Cretan origin; Metapontum, said to have been founded by the father of one of the companions of Nestor, king of Pylos, as well as Usentum and Buxentum. Greece and the Aegean have place-names in *-nthos* associated in trade with Crete, while similar names occur in Caria. These and other places in south Italy may thus have been trading-posts in close touch with Crete or with its daughter cities on the mainland of Greece, such as Argos, Tiryns, Corinth, or Pylos.

We may imagine, therefore, that while Knossos flourished,

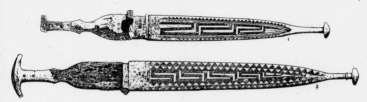

FIG. 34. Iron swords from Torre Galli, Calabria.

and after its downfall while commerce was active in Mycenean Greece, trade relations with Italy were sustained; after the Mycenean cities fell, and the later Achaean power collapsed before the invading Dorians, such trade passed into other hands, perhaps to the Lydians, whose thalassocracy or command of the sea is placed by Eusebius between 1172 and 1080 B.C. This was about the time that iron arrived in Italy, and at this time the Lydians had inherited what was left of the trade of the Hittite Empire, which had fallen before the Phrygian invaders about 1200 B.C.

It seems likely, then, that the knowledge of iron was brought from Lydia to commercial ports of south Italy that had afore-time traded with the Cretans, and there is some slight evidence that one of these was Tarentum. Some thirty years ago a bronze sledge-hammer was found near Taranto amid Late Bronze Age surroundings; this is the earliest sledge-hammer known, and such hammers were needed for working iron.

Iron tools seem to have spread rapidly through the peninsula, though in small quantities, and before long a very specialized industry arose in Calabria. It seems likely that among those who brought the new metal from Lydia were the Tyrrhenians, whose movements we are about to describe, and it may have been the presence of iron in the Isle of Elba that ultimately drew them northwards.

The various stages of the Villanova culture have been found at the hamlet of Villanova, about five miles from Bologna: these are called:

Benacci I	.	.	1050–900 B.C.
Benacci II	.	.	900–700 B.C.
Arnoaldi	.	.	700–500 B.C.
Certosa	.	.	500– B.C.

The last, which is Etruscan, will be discussed later.

The ashes of the dead were contained in biconical urns, decorated with geometric designs not unlike those on contemporary Greek vases, and covered with bowl-shaped lids. The accompanying articles give a good idea of the civilization of the time. The first Benacci period had bronze armlets and ear-rings. Fine bronze bits, sometimes ornamented with a bronze figurine of a horse at either end, imply that some of the men were horsemen, while a bronze staff from one tomb, surmounted by the model of a running dog, shows us that this animal was kept, probably for hunting. Swords, spears, and axes are also found, but not in great profusion.

In the second Benacci period feminine ornaments are more abundant and the tombs give evidence of greater wealth. Iron implements now become much commoner, as do glass and amber. This indicates trade both with central Europe and, during the latter half of this period, with new arrivals on the coast to the south.

During the Arnoaldi period the Northern Villanovans grew much more prosperous, partly, it may be surmised, from trade with central Europe, for the evidence of commercial dealings with their neighbours across the Apennines is very slight. Iron

Fig. 35. Villanovan pottery.

became abundant and was used prodigally; enormous pike-heads over a foot long were made, iron axes were common, and iron swords were not unusual. Chariots, with iron tyres, came into use, while glass and amber occur in profusion. The artistic spirit, however, shows marked signs of decay.

The earliest evidence of Southern Villanovans seems to ante-date the oldest tombs at Villanova by fifty or a hundred years;

MacIver dates to the eleventh or possibly to the twelfth century B.C. early settlements probably of pastoralists in the mountainous district of Telfa in Tuscany and in the Alban Hills, while a small cemetery uncovered by Boni in the Forum at Rome appears to be almost contemporary.

Northern and Southern Villanovans did not differ materially in the first Benacci period, but in the south in place of the

FIG. 36. Hut urns of the Southern Villanova culture.

northern biconical urns they made funerary urns in the form of the huts in which they dwelt, circular, with a conical thatched roof, supported on a structure of wattle and daub, sometimes having a porch with wooden pillars; but a slightly later bronze model from Falerii shows a rectangular timber-framed house with a roof apparently resting on rafters that crossed one another at the ridge. Towards the end of the first Benacci period fresh influences of the Etruscans arrived, materially changing the civilization on this side of the Apennines, and ultimately, in the Certosa period, having a like effect around Bologna.

In Chapter 3 of this volume we have mentioned a story told by Herodotus of the departure from Smyrna about 1200 B.C. of some Tyrsenians from Lydia. There are reasons for suspecting that they went to Thrace and the island of Lemnos. Later, according to Herodotus, they settled in Italy, in the land of the Ombricoi, in whom we may recognize the Umbrians, at that time occupying Tuscany as well as a part of what later was Umbria. MacIver, on archaeological evidence, says they arrived in Tuscany just before 800 B.C., evidently by sea, since their first settlements were by the coast at Tarquinii, Caere, and Vetulonia, from which they spread over the province known after them as Etruria. We have already hinted that earlier they may have traded with Tarentum and adjacent ports.

It is possible that these Tyrsenians or Tyrrhenians were one of the many groups in Lydia at that time, but one of us hazarded another explanation some years ago. It will be remembered that in Chapter 11 of *The Steppe and the Sown,* and again in Chapter 11 of *The Way of the Sea,* we mentioned the existence in Asia Minor of certain colonies of Sumerian traders. There is no reason to believe that they ceased to exist there until the downfall of the Hittite Empire about 1200 B.C., when some, at least, are likely to have moved into Lydia, the only part of that empire that escaped the onrush of the Phrygian hordes. Here they would be commercial rivals of the trading Lydians. This, rather than famine, may well have caused them to look for new homes and fresh markets, while the newly discovered metal would provide material for their trading ventures.

The Sumerians lived in city-states, or cities with only a small adjacent territory. The Etruscans lived in similar city-states, and Etruria was not so much a state as a loose confederacy of twelve or more independent city-states. The Sumerian city-state was governed by a magistrate, with some religious status, known as Patesi or Ishakku; each Etruscan city was also under the rule of a religious magistrate, known as a Lucumo, an office once filled by Lars Porsena of Clusium. Lastly the Sumerians were given to the practice of hepatoscopy, or interpreting the future from the study of the liver of a sheep. Models of such sheep's livers were made in bronze or earthenware, and the surface was divided into squares, each with its appropriate sign. The only three such models yet discovered were found, one at Babylon, another at Boghaz Keui, the site of the Hittite capital, and the third, of Etruscan make, near Piacenza (see Fig. 14, p. 45).

Arrived in Tuscany the Tyrrhenians founded a number of cities, first on the coast and later inland, until the federation included twelve and later fourteen or more. Probably they did not to any extent displace the Ombricoi or Umbrians, who seem to have been living in the rural districts many centuries later, any more than these Umbrians had displaced the former peasant population that had been there since neolithic days. It appears to us likely that the three groups settled down together, the Umbrians as a military and hunting aristocratic class of landowners, the Tyrrhenians forming groups of city merchants, while the aborigines tilled the land for their Umbrian lords or dwelt in the slums of the Tyrrhenian cities.

The population of Tuscany had long been very mixed. A few years ago the Abbé Calzoni discovered at Belverde on the mountain of Cetona a settlement that had lasted during the greater part of the Bronze Age down to the beginning of the Villanova period. Much skeletal material was found, but the bones had been separated and reinterred, so we have no description of complete skeletons, nor do we know the relative antiquity of the remains. Of the skulls measured, eight had length-breadth indices ranging between 75 and 79, while eleven had indices ranging from 80 to 86; many of the latter had heads somewhat higher than is usual in western Europe. The stature of the men ranged from 5 feet 8½ inches to 4 feet 9½ inches, and of fifty-eight of these, nineteen were more than 5 feet 5 inches high while six were less than 5 feet; only a few women reached 5 feet 6 inches.

The later population of Tuscany included individuals with long and others with broad heads, and there has been considerable difference of opinion as to how this evidence should be interpreted. Sergi has claimed that the long-headed stock were of the Mediterranean race; Wilser and Woltman think them Nordic, the latter mentioning that relatively blond hair is portrayed in some Etruscan tomb frescoes. There is, we believe, some truth in both statements, though it is difficult to produce convincing evidence until a larger number of measurements have been published. The whole of Italy seems first to have been inhabited by people of the Mediterranean race, and a large number of modern Tuscans conform to that type.

The statement of Woltman about blondness cannot, however, be neglected. An Orvieto tomb known as *dei sette Camini* is attributed to the fourth century B.C. and has a fresco, admirably reproduced in a replica of the tomb set up in the garden of the Museum at Florence; a man is sitting holding a spear and wearing a head-dress made of the head of a wolf. This man is usually believed to represent Pluto, who is figured in similar attire in the *Tomba Golini* at the same place and in the *Grotta dell'Orco* at Corneto. There is this difference, however, that in the *Grotta dell'Orco* the figure of Pluto, inscribed AITA, has a deep red skin and a black beard, while that in the *Tomba Golini*, inscribed EITA, has a red complexion and beard of a still deeper red, and the figure in the *Tomba dei setti Camini* has a reddish-brown skin, reddish wavy hair, and a dark brown beard.

Even if these scenes represent life in the underworld they are clearly copied from earthly models. As Helbig has pointed out, the frescoes in the *Grotta dell'Orco* either are by a Greek artist, or at any rate show the spirit of Greek art; those at Orvieto are more of a native character and show Pluto with relatively blond traits; Persephone in the *Tomba Golini* is of fair complexion and has light hair, while in the neighbouring *Tomba*

delle due Bighe a woman reveller, inscribed Thannkvil or Tana-
quil, is shown with golden hair. There was thus a blond element
in the population, especially in the upper class.

Some Warrior Tombs are possibly as early as the ninth century, though few go back earlier than 800 B.C. The most primitive type of grave is the *tomba à pozzo*, a well-like structure
enlarged at the base to contain a sepulchral urn. Later this
recess was extended with a roof of barrel vaulting to hold a
burial and still later the graves were covered with often elaborate
mounds or tumuli. Unlike other of the richer Etruscan families
who buried their dead in large chambered vaults for many
generations, the warrior was buried in a single grave, though
occasionally an adjoining chamber held the body of his wife.
Such graves have been found near most of the cities in Etruria,
the best known being the Regulini-Galássi tomb at Cervetri,
dating from the seventh or eighth century B.C. Unfortunately
the bones, on admission of the outside air, so we are told,
crumbled into dust, but are said to have belonged to very tall
men, and one grave opened in 1826 at Monte Rozzi near Corneto
is said to have held two sarcophagi, one containing a giant and
the other his horse.

The Iron Age population of Etruria was thus very mixed,
each component playing a different role in the economy of the
country. The pastoral people, Umbrians and others, who introduced the Villanova culture, came, we believe, from the slopes
of the eastern Alps and were tall and robust, with relatively long
heads and blond colouring. They spoke an Indo-European
tongue and became rural landowners on the mountain sides. At
first they cremated their dead like the Northern Villanovans,
and placed the ashes in hut-urns at the bottom of deep well-
like pits. Later they interred the remains of their dead, fully
extended and clothed in armour, in rectangular graves or sarcophagi, covered with a mound of earth or masonry.

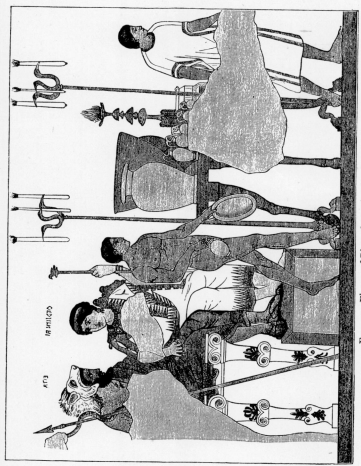

FIG. 37. Figure of Pluto from the *Tomba Golini.*

Later on, about 820 B.C., there arrived the Tyrrhenians, ultimately from Asia Minor. These, we imagine, were men of medium height, thick-set, broad-headed, short-necked, and often stout, the *Etruscus obesus* of Catullus. They were urban traders on the lower lands cultivated by aboriginal serfs. Normally they cremated and at one time placed the ashes in elaborately carved sarcophagi of alabaster, upon which reposed a representation of the deceased. Finally the aboriginal, long-headed brunets of Mediterranean type, with some admixture of broad-headed elements that had come southward from the Alps, seem to have served both sets of masters, on the land and in the mines.

About the middle of the eighth century (the traditional date is 753 B.C.) some members of a pastoral tribe from the Alban Mountains came down and made a little settlement on one of the small hills that fringe the left bank of the Tiber, perhaps in self-defence. The tribes on the Alban Mountain were closely allied and spoke the Latin dialect, and the land that they occupied stretched to the Tiber. The Tyrrhenians were occupying all the lands beyond the river and had already drawn as close as Veii, only a few miles distant. It has been thought that the Latin settlement on the Tiber, known then as now by the name of Roma, was placed there as an outpost to defend the easiest crossing of the river, for here a long island lies in the middle of the stream. The hill upon which they first settled was square with a flat top, and on this they erected a temple to Pales, the goddess of their flocks; this hill was known later as the *Mons Palatinus*. Soon afterwards they took possession of another hill, with precipitous sides, upon which they fixed their *arx* or refuge against times of danger; this was afterwards known as *Mons Capitolinus*. Later on they spread out downstream, and included another hill, the *Mons Aventinus*, and about the same time placed a fortress on a hill across the river, to act as a bridge-

head; this was known as the *Janiculum*. In the meantime the
original Latin settlers had coalesced with a kindred group, called
the Sabines, who dwelt on the *Mons Quirinalis*, and it is said

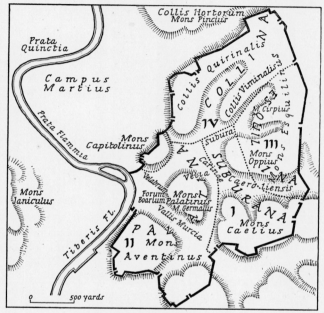

FIG. 38. Map of the site of Rome.

that they had also incorporated a group of Etruscans, who were
occupying the *Mons Caelius*.

Thus came Rome into existence and for more than a century
its inhabitants kept the Etruscans at bay, but at length these
enterprising traders, making use, we can well believe, of the
martial qualities of their Umbrian colleagues, took Rome, placed
a Lucumo named Tarquinius in charge, and gradually annexed
all the territory beyond as far as the Greek colonies near Naples.

Later, leaving the fierce mountain tribes like the Samnites severely alone, the Etruscan warriors crossed the Apennines behind Fiesole and conquered the territory of the Northern Villanovans in the plain beyond about 525 B.C., destroying the settlement at Villanova and erecting near by a new city, Felsina, for the Tyrrhenian merchants. Soon the whole of the Po valley was added to their dominion.

While the Etruscan warriors were on these northern adventures the excesses of Tarquinius Superbus, the Lucumo at Rome, incensed the people, who drove him and his sons out of the city, in which they set up a republic. The expelled Tarquins endeavoured to arouse the Etruscans, and Porsena, the Lucumo of Clusium, summoned them to follow him to Rome. The best of the warriors were, however, in the Po valley and the expedition proved a failure. For more than a century constant war was waged between the Etruscan confederacy and the city of Rome, reinforced after 493 B.C. by a league of the Latin states. In 474 B.C. the Etruscan fleet was defeated by the Greeks off Cumae and early in the next century the Romans took Veii and razed it to the ground, while about the same time a vast horde of Gauls entered the Po valley and brought Etruscan domination there to an end. Etruscan rule was henceforth confined to Etruria proper, the modern Tuscany, into which the Romans had already penetrated, and which was conquered by Cornelius Dolabella in 283 B.C.

Not until 91 B.C. were the inhabitants of the Etruscan cities granted Roman citizenship, but many Tyrrhenians had settled in Rome much earlier, and had set up as goldsmiths or bankers in a street at the foot of the Capitol, leading from the Forum to the river, for this street became known as the *Via Etrusca*. Several of the great Tyrrhenian families were well represented in Rome and became plebeian *gentes*, and one such, from Clusium, produced several well-known politicians. In Chiusi a tomb shows a number of inscriptions relating to a family bearing the name of Lekne, and one of these inscriptions is bilingual and in this Lekne is translated Licinius. In Rome the plebeian *gens*, Licinia, included many distinguished families, such as those of Crassus, Lucullus, and Murena. C. Licinius Calvus, tribune from 376 to 367 B.C., introduced a number of laws in favour of the plebeians, including one enabling a member of this class to be elected as consul. Six other laws were subsequently introduced by members of this *gens*. It is clear that from this time on the Etruscan, or perhaps we should say Tyrrhenian, element was important politically at Rome, and this may account for an apparent change in the psychology of the Roman people during the third century B.C. that has been noted by more than one historian.

BOOKS

RANDALL-MACIVER, D. *Villanovans and Early Etruscans* (Oxford, 1924).
RANDALL-MACIVER, D. *The Iron Age in Italy* (Oxford, 1927).
RANDALL-MACIVER, D. *The Etruscans* (Oxford, 1927).
RANDALL-MACIVER, D. *Italy before the Romans* (Oxford, 1928).

10

Iron in Central Europe

IN Chapters 7 and 9 of *The Horse and the Sword* we referred at some length to the culture which, before the beginning of the last millennium B.C., became characteristic of the Lausitz area, situated on the loess between the Elbe and the Oder, and we described the associated customs of cremating the dead and of burying the urns, sometimes without protection, in large cemeteries or urn-fields. We described, too, the spread of this culture through Hungary to the northern shore of the Aegean Sea, as well as its westward extension to what are now south Germany,

Switzerland, and France. This was a time of warm dry summers, and the grain-growers were moving in search of patches of rich land. In the meantime improvements took place in the strains of wheat sown, salt became of importance in the diet of the grain-growers, while the use of the horse became commoner. Travelling bronze-smiths were at this time supplying metal goods to communities living far away from the mines over which they kept control, and carried far afield the leaf-shaped sword, the *fibula*, and the socketed axe.

It was into such a world that the use of iron crept, as it were, and it is becoming increasingly clear that it is no longer possible to draw a sharp dividing line between the ages of bronze and iron. The new metal appeared at first as a rare commodity, as we gather from the account in the *Iliad* of the games celebrated at the funeral of Patroclus; for some centuries many objects of daily use continued to be made of bronze. It was only by a short space of time that the spread of the use of iron preceded a number of other changes. Chief among these were an increase in the rainfall accompanied by cooler summers throughout Europe and adjacent areas, the greater power and enterprise of the Aegean and Italian peoples during the dawn of what is known as the classical age, the increased use of salt by the peoples of central Europe, and a number of other factors to be described later. It is these, rather than the use of iron, that primarily distinguish this period from what went before. Later in the Iron Age this metal was much more frequently used, though bronze *fibulae* were increasingly made and were apparently traded far and wide.

The features enumerated above have long made it convenient to divide the Iron Age of pre-Roman times, as far as central and western Europe are concerned, into two phases; the earlier of these is named after the salt centre at Hallstatt in Austria, where a large cemetery of this period was discovered in 1846, while the

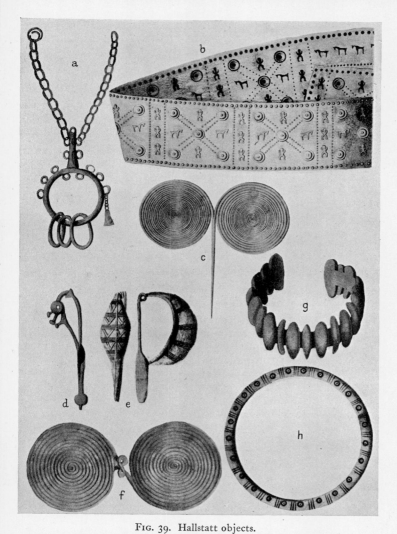

FIG. 39. Hallstatt objects.

a, Personal ornament. b, Belt, with figures. c, Double-spiral pin. d, e, Fibulae. f, Spectacle fibula, specially characteristic. g, Penannular rings. h, Complete rings.

later phase has been called after the settlement at La Tène on Lake Neuchâtel in Switzerland. During the earlier phase iron was much less commonly used than in the later, and, in many areas, there was a lower standard of living as well. During the later phase echoes from the classical world reverberate on all sides.

The study of the Hallstatt phase of culture in central Europe has profited greatly from the work of Reinecke, whose inferences are largely used in this chapter. How much of the earliest stage of the Hallstatt culture should be reckoned as within the Bronze Age can never be decided; the continuity in south Germany is absolute. In *Merchant Venturers in Bronze*, on page 61, we mentioned that some people, who seem to have arrived at an earlier date from the grasslands of south-east Russia, had reached the upland districts lying to the west of Silesia. They appear to have been living in a pastoral condition and possessed extensive flocks and herds. They buried their dead beneath barrows or tumuli, and are usually known as the Tumuli people. These herdsmen first appeared on the German uplands early in the Middle Bronze Age, and, as we mentioned in *The Horse and the Sword*, page 104, towards the close of that period had spread over much of the hill country of southern Germany and the eastern Alpine region. By some it is believed that these Tumuli people were the ancestors of those known later as Illyrians, but others think, with greater probability, that their descendants were not only the Illyrians but the Venetians, Celts, and perhaps those who later spoke some of the Italic dialects. Early in the Hallstatt period these Tumuli people were occupying a large part of the uplands of south Germany and the adjoining regions, to some extent ousting the grain-growers of the urn-fields and Lausitz culture, who continued cultivating the richer patches of soil in the lowlands north of the Neckar, in south Germany, while they spread north of the Main towards the central hill country of Germany and towards the middle and lower Rhine.

These two peoples, those of the Tumuli and those of the Urn-fields, seem to have mingled to some extent, for sometimes skeletons are found, buried instead of burned, accompanied by weapons of the Tumuli culture. The Urnfield tradition is shown in ossuaries of urn or bucket form containing ashes and occasional metal fragments as well as large collections of small vessels, such as urns, dishes, plates, beakers, and cups. The ossuary was enclosed by dry-walling, consisting of stone slabs or planks, and, over this covering, earth was heaped to form a low mound, often surrounded by stones. The urn-fields were the habitations of the dead, gathered together in large numbers, apparently like the contemporary villages of the living. These houses or huts were heaped together without order, and each was as a rule rectangular and built of blocks, or of timber-framing filled in with wattle-and-daub.

The relationship of this culture to that found on the northern slopes of the Alpine region, in which iron was used only for decorating sword-handles and such objects, is obviously close. In the northern Alpine region the pile-dwellings of the Late Bronze Age were, in fact, remaining in use, with only slight changes due to the influence of iron-using peoples. They represent, in the main, a fusion of the urn-fields culture with an older indigenous civilization belonging to lake villages of the second series so important in the Swiss Late Bronze Age. We thus find in Switzerland during the Hallstatt phase a lingering of old cultures, analogous to the lingering of the Late Neolithic culture in the lake villages of the older series contemporary with the Early Bronze Age elsewhere.

After a while the Hallstatt phase of culture penetrated Switzerland as far as the lakes in the cantons of Berne and Fribourg, where a good deal of gold-leaf ornament has been found; it reached Lake Thun, but apparently failed to pass the Bernese Oberland to Lake Geneva, while most of the west of Switzerland remained more true to the old ways. This period, in spite of the introduction of a certain amount of fresh blood and culture into Switzerland, witnessed a severe general decline in that country, a decline associated with the change of climate from warmer and drier to cooler and wetter. Almost contemporary with the Hallstatt phase in the northern cantons, extensions of culture from the Po basin possessing occasional articles from farther north reached the canton of Ticino. In canton Valais, however, we find little of this kind; that region, like Savoy and parts of the Jura, may almost be said to have remained in the Bronze Age until it was affected by Roman influences. This is all the more surprising since the La Tène culture is named from a station just beneath the Jura, in which the later stages of that culture are richly exemplified.

It was from south Germany that the urn-fields culture spread to Burgundy, Champagne, and the central parts of the Paris basin, where swords of Hallstatt type and bronze razors occur, as will be discussed later; in this direction, however, the intruding influence was relatively temporary and the tradition of the Middle Bronze Age seems, for the most part, to have re-established its sway. Tumuli, of the phases before, during, and after they were influenced by the urn-fields, are extremely numerous in Burgundy and in parts of the Paris basin.

The eastern or Austrian Alps, like those of Switzerland, reveal a lake-village culture of the end of the Neolithic Age or of the Early Bronze Age; these remained in a neolithic phase, though the opener loess-floored lands of Lower Austria acquired a bronze culture related to that of Aunjetitz described in our seventh volume, *Merchant Venturers in Bronze*. About the middle of the Bronze Age, when the tumulus-builders were dominant in south Germany, the mountain country of Austria seems to have been almost empty, but in the Late Bronze Age a great change occurred. Chance finds show that, ere the neolithic phase had passed away in the highlands, the Alpine passes, even the high ones, were coming into use, and that men were seeking refuge among the heights against warlike pressure from below in the Bronze Age.

Some authors have thought that copper and salt were mined in the Austrian Alps from the dawn of the Bronze Age, but Mahr, whose little guide to Hallstatt is invaluable, while giving

FIG. 40. Hallstatt swords.

details of the discoveries of stone axes to the number of seven on the Salzberg at Hallstatt, wisely urges that, in spite of the discovery of one stone tool in the Emperor Joseph's gallery, there is no proof that mining was carried on at that date. He even hints that the stone implements may have been brought there in later times 'for luck'. There are clear indications that a way through the mountains along the side of the Traun river was in use during the Late Bronze Age, in which Hallstatt began to develop that importance which made it one of the most famous of prehistoric sites.

Picturesquely situated on the Aussee, its Salzberg is rich in deposits of salt of the Triassic period, and it is this product that was responsible for the fame of Hallstatt and its large increase of population during the early part of the last millennium B.C.

A number of bronze finds, including a hoard found in 1830 and melted down, may even be a little older, and in these there are sickles, stop-ridged, winged, and socketed axes, arrow-heads, arm-rings, a bronze sword, pins, lance-points, and other objects. These, in such an area, may well date from the very end of the Bronze Age, and herald the great development that was to take place.

The great prehistoric cemetery of Hallstatt must once have contained 2,000 to 2,500 burials, but unfortunately the majority were destroyed or only superficially investigated, and finds from them are scattered the world over. The graves are hardly tumuli; but they must have been marked in some way, for only occasionally do newer ones interfere with the older; more often they fit between them. They often lie in calcareous rubble under the humus, but sometimes in the humus itself; the body or ashes may be covered with stone blocks, and many of the bodies face east. 455 cremations and 525 burials have been fully identified, while 13 show partial burning. There are 179 bronze finds definitely associated with 67 cremations, but only 3 with 525 burials. The former include daggers and swords of bronze, but any iron associated with these is only in the form of small knives. The burials, on the other hand, have iron axes and lances, amber, and even importations of glass from the south. Reinecke's view, supported by Mahr, is that the burials are in the main later than the cremations. The ashes in the cremation burials were rarely placed in urns, but apparently the pots in the graves served to hold offerings of food and drink; unfortunately vast numbers of these pots were long ago destroyed. The spectacle-like *fibulae* in the burials are also found in west Hungary, Croatia, Slavonia, and farther south with stray specimens even in Greece; they are unknown from north and mid-Italy, but common enough on the Adriatic coasts from Picenum to Sicily. They have been held to be the best indicators of a people that is supposed to have spread about east central Europe in the early part of the last millennium B.C. Hallstatt is probably the most important site for this type of *fibula*.

Along with the evidence from the great cemetery we have that from the mining galleries which were apparently propped up by woodwork and illuminated by burning bundles of sticks or chips. Ventilation as well as movement must have been difficult, while the salt would doubtless quickly attack the tools, as has been proved in connexion with salt-mining at Hallstatt since A.D. 1311. The finds in mining galleries all belong to the early part of the period represented in the cemeteries, that early part being provisionally dated by Hoernes as from 900 to 700 B.C.; one might even add that the mining galleries yield finds only of the first part of this period, so that mining for salt apparently ceased not far from 800 B.C. Mahr has some valuable reflections on this point. The mining galleries were apparently much troubled by falls of the roof, and the parts of the floor subsequently pro-tected by these falls are remarkably free from water-runnels. He thence argues that mining was carried on in a dry period, and, in *The Horse and the Sword*, we have repeatedly argued for a period of warm dry climate before, and perhaps for some time after, 1000 B.C. He suggests further that at some time after 900 B.C., perhaps about 800 B.C., the climate became cooler and moister, and so made it easier for the industry to dissolve the salt out with the help of the numerous springs that must have developed under the new conditions. The incoming of the people who buried their dead and used less bronze and more iron may also have promoted the change of method. Grave-finds are less common among the burials than among the cremations, and it has been argued that this was a period of impoverish-ment at Hallstatt as well as in many other parts of Europe, in which burial often tends to replace cremation from about 800 or 700 B.C. onwards.

The second phase of activity at Hallstatt continued for some centuries, until objects belonging to the La Tène culture began to arrive, probably about 400 B.C. This is the period of marked

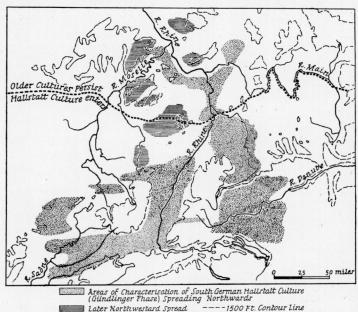

Areas of Characterisation of South German Hallstatt Culture (Gündlinger Phase) Spreading Northwards

Later Northwestard Spread   – – – – 1500 Ft. Contour Line

FIG. 41. Map of north-westward spread of Hallstatt culture in S. Germany.

unrest and of Celtic conquest, and somehow it involved the cessation of activity at Hallstatt; it was only in a late La Tène phase, about 100 B.C., that this activity was renewed. Hallstatt thus yields mainly objects dating from between the end of the Bronze Age and the spread of La Tène culture. It is, therefore, most appropriate that its name should have been given to the early phase of the prehistoric Iron Age, during which iron was obviously much scarcer than in the La Tène phase. Bronze *antennae*-swords mark the earliest stages and are succeeded by the Hallstatt sword, at first in bronze and then in iron, sometimes with an ivory pommel. Daggers are common and may be gold-plated, while some later specimens are ornamented with pearls. Axes of bronze and of iron or of both, helmets, and what may be fragments of shields are known. A bucket-cover, clearly belonging to the second phase, is ornamented with realistic as well as with mythical animals, and the style has come from the Aegean or from Asia Minor, probably through Etruscan territory. Some much cruder decoration on another bucket-cover may well be a local effort to copy a fine piece of foreign work. Glass was imported towards the end of the period.

Perhaps a final reflection on Hallstatt may be permitted. We see in the early part of the last millennium B.C. a spread of stock-raising and, it would seem, some reduction of cultivation. At the same time salt acquires a great importance, apparently rather suddenly. Is it going too far to suggest that the making of a provision of salt meat for the winter may have been becoming the widespread practice that it has been during most of the subsequent centuries?

Hallstatt itself has been discussed with as much detail as space permits because of its special importance and of the fact that general accounts are not readily available. In the great days of mining there its inhabitants were apparently already part of a population that was spreading over central Europe, and Reinecke has discussed the cultural accompaniment of this spread in terms of stages named from sites in south Germany. The first of these is that of transition, in Danubian Germany, from the cultivators who made urn-fields to the stock-keeping peoples, who largely replaced them in that region but apparently remained less important farther north.

The second is called the Gündling stage, with a further spread of stock-raising apparently in the ninth and eighth centuries B.C.

The pottery flasks of this stage, some with handles, are often thin and of fine grain, well polished and decorated with painting in red, yellow, or black patterns, suggesting connexions with the eastern and south-eastern Alps. Stepped dishes are another feature of this stage. Both cremations and burials occur, and food and drink containers were very generally placed with the dead; some fine bronze swords have been found with these. The people concerned, still obviously retaining a good deal of connexion or kinship with the older indigenous elements, spread across south Germany westwards to south Baden, Alsace, the Pfalz, and eastern France, but their ideas did not entirely replace earlier fashions.

FIG. 42. *Kerbschnitt* pottery.

The third stage is named from the Alb and Koberstadt, and is especially interesting because it shows a revival in East France and Germany, south of the Danube, of the custom of burial and of the use of painting combined with the *Kerbschnitt* scheme of decorating pottery, which was a feature of the tumulus phase of the Middle Bronze Age discussed in Chapter 5 of *Merchant Venturers in Bronze*. *Kerbschnitt* is a scheme of deeply impressed ornament derived from wood-carving models and it aims at producing an effect by the addition of light and shade to a pattern that is often linear and angular. The *Kerbschnitt* ornament of Bronze Age pottery was developed in an unbroken band around the pot; in Iron Age pottery this is usually not the case, as Fig. 42 indicates. Farther north the use of *Kerbschnitt* is rarer, and, in this stage, the eastern Alpine styles of pottery painting are more conspicuous and elaborate north of the German Danube than they are in the south. Apparently, therefore, there was a certain added penetration of the stock-raising peoples northward at this stage, including probably the eighth and seventh centuries B.C., leaving perhaps the lands nearer the Alps to some extent to a revival of old ways, very likely through intermarriage with indigenous women. It seems that, though the northward movement was successful, the old cultivating peoples remained strong in the country to the west of the middle Rhine. The region south of the German Danube appears to have been the most prosperous, very likely because it was less disturbed by movements. In this stage, both south and north of the German Danube, long iron swords as well as lances and knives were widely in use, with fine two-edged daggers in addition in the south. Westwards, in France, swords were still of bronze, though the bronze sword had by this time almost disappeared farther east. Horse-trappings are another feature of this stage.

The fourth, or Mehren, stage shows still further advance of stock-raising elements over the higher lands of middle Germany, east Lorraine, the Eifel, and other western districts, but the old cultivating peoples obviously held their own in the loess-floored lowlands near Mainz. It would be going too far to maintain the name east-Alpine or Illyrian for the stock-raisers advancing during this stage. That there were among them descendants of these older conquerors seems clear, but apparently there were also elements from north Germany with distinctive cultural features, notably bronze neck- or head-rings of the *Wendelring* type. Painted pottery with linear patterns is highly characteristic of this stage.

We retain a general picture of stock-raisers moving from the south-east and east through south and central Germany, stage by stage, and mixing, as they moved, with what German writers think was a Celtic-speaking population. This language question will be discussed in a later chapter.

As the stock-raisers advanced, the regions behind them showed the usual, and in the end profitable, fusion of conquerors and conquered, while some areas of good soil and climate with old-settled populations, such as the Mainz basin, for a time resisted conquest and so tended rather to add newly assimilated features to their older civilizations than to change fundamentally. The change to a cooler and wetter climate, to which reference has been made, may have been an important factor in the spread of stock-raisers at the expense of cultivators. The fineness of the pottery of the former is a little surprising until one realizes that they came from the south-eastern ends of the Alps and also must have taken to themselves the women-potters of their predecessors.

Towards the north-east there survived the civilization known by the name of Lausitz and discussed in Chapter 7 of *The Horse and the Sword*, and, as it had given rise to the urn-fields culture, there were developed sequences of styles in ornamentation of pottery on the German plains. The Aurith type (about 1000–800 B.C.) has been distinguished by its decoration with rows of punch-marks associated with lines or grooves and by the yellow or red colour of the pottery. The Göritz type, next in seniority (800–500 B.C.), near the northern frontier of the Lausitz cultures, and more widely spread to the west, still used punch-marks as well as lines which are mainly cord impressions but also lines in zig-zags probably derived from the zigzags of colour on the painted pottery established already long before this time in regions to the south-east as has been stated in several volumes of this series. The Billendorf type is a more elegant variant of the Göritz, and is found chiefly in the area immediately to the south of that of the Göritz. It is perhaps the Göritz type that had most influence on the pottery of the Hallstatt phase generally. In addition to this, however, one finds, in central Europe and especially in the Danube basin in Hungary and Bavaria, pottery ornamented with semi-realistic incised drawings, for example a four-wheeled chariot drawn by a pair of horses, with a man riding in front and one walking behind.

It is noteworthy that, whereas, in the western Mediterranean in the first half of the last millennium B.C., culture contacts with the Aegean, as well as a revival of adequate rainfall, promoted group life and spread the idea of the city, in central Europe, in spite of the growth of the amber trade, this did not occur. Herdsmen on the move, and a cool damp climate, were doubtless hindrances to evolution on these lines, and in these circumstances culture borrowings from the Aegean were not of much importance; in fact in the early stages, as mentioned in Chapters 4, 6, and 7 of *The Horse and the Sword*, elements from east central Europe were actually spreading to the Aegean. The westward movements discussed in this chapter followed these in time, and it seems likely that they were prompted in part by the westward advances of the Scythians from the south Russian steppe discussed in Chapter 1 of this volume.

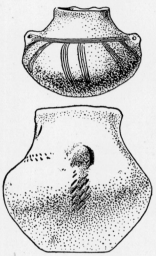

FIG. 43. Göritz pottery.

An article by de Navarro in the *Geographical Journal* for December 1925 gives a good account of prehistoric trade in northern amber. The western shores of Jutland were the first source, and the material was widely used for ornaments by the people of the late Neolithic period in Denmark. Cremation, introduced in the Bronze Age, makes it impossible to say whether the custom of placing amber necklaces with the dead was

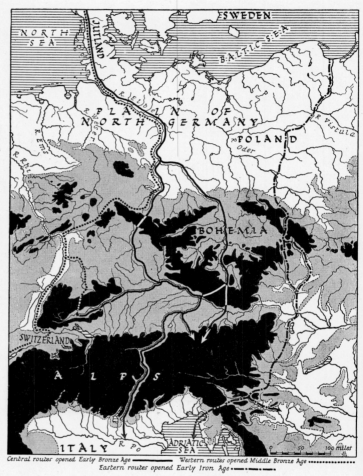

Central routes opened Early Bronze Age ——— Western routes opened Middle Bronze Age ···········
Eastern routes opened Early Iron Age ·—·—·—·

FIG. 44. Map of amber routes.

continued, but in the Early Bronze Age amber was reaching Aunjetitz in Bohemia in fair quantity, no doubt up the Elbe. It also began to be traded into Bavaria by a route farther west, probably using the river Saale for some distance. Reaching the Alps by the one or the other way, it was carried over the Brenner Pass to the Terremare settlements of the Po basin. Later in the Bronze Age a route from the Saale through mid-Germany westwards to the Rhine, branching up the Rhine, Neckar, and Aar became important, while, by a more eastern route, amber reached Mycenae. In the Hallstatt phase of the Early Iron Age the beaches of the east Prussian region began to be exploited and the miners' cemeteries at Hallstatt have yielded quantities, chiefly from the ninth- and eighth-century graves. The Alps and north Italy lost their connexion with the trade which, in a period of cold and precipitation, came to use chiefly the eastern side of the Alps, and so reached Fiume at the head of the Adriatic. In the La Tène phase, to be discussed below, the trade in northern amber temporarily declined very seriously, and glass, coral, and enamel came into fashion, but the Etruscans liked amber and got it. In connexion with the diminution of the amber trade in late Hallstatt and La Tène times it is also to be remembered that the Scythian invasion westward along the loess belt north of the Carpathians may have interfered with the trade route which it crossed. The amber trade revived once more in the days of Imperial Rome.

As the Hallstatt phase was reaching its end, classical ideas and fashions were spreading in Italy and southern France and began to reach the south of Germany. The next phase is named from La Tène, a river-bank station at the north-east end of Lake Neuchâtel, though that settlement yields objects only of the second and third divisions of this phase. La Tène I, not represented at this site but very important in south Germany and north France, is a transitional stage from the Hallstatt fashions to newer styles showing classical influences modified by local ideas. In this transition, simple geometric or zoomorphic designs were less common and elaborate ornament based upon the leaf and the flower or stylized palmette became abundant. In contradistinction to Greek styles, however, that of La Tène shows an effort less to give an idea of symmetrical design based on plant structure than to fill the space available with elaborate schemes of curves. Coins copied from those of Philip of Macedon appear before the end of La Tène II, and during this stage the use of iron seems to have become far more general. To older modes of fine decoration in bronze is added the piercing of metal in elaborate patterns. The workers of the La Tène period loved colour and used coral inlay, later evolving the idea of coloured enamel, which will be referred to in the chapter on western Europe. La Tène itself seems to have been a fortified station and military depot rather than a normal habitation site, and its position shows that it is in no sense a continuation of the idea of the Lake Villages. These died out during the period of transition from bronze to iron.

Many opinions have been held as to the Early Iron Age in Baltic Europe. Sophus Müller considers that, just as a Stone Age with some infiltration of bronze persisted in the north for some time after the Bronze Age developed farther south, so the Bronze Age with some infiltration of iron persisted in the north until after 600 B.C., that is to say until the Hallstatt phase of central Europe was nearing its end. This lingering Bronze Age showed decline in style and a tendency to excessive ornament. The old view that it lasted into Roman or even post-Roman times has now been abandoned. When iron spread more definitely northwards it came with its attendant fashions through Westphalia and Schleswig-Holstein to Jutland and Norway as well as from the Oder-Vistula district through Bornholm to Denmark and Sweden. Though considerable skill was shown and bog iron was brought into use, there was little local development of style and finds do not reach far north in the Scandinavian peninsula. The deterioration of climate is probably largely responsible for this.

Reference has already been made to the complete decline at Hallstatt about 400 B.C. when also north Silesia, north Poland, and Finland were very poor. The very cold phase was passing away by this time and probably hill-slopes in Austria were suffering from torrents due to melting snow and ice, while the flat clay-lands of the other regions named would be troubled with water, marsh, and forest, conditions more favourable to wild beasts than to man. Bohemia with its well-drained loess soil and consequent relative freedom from forest, as well as its trading activities, was less hampered in this way.

On the other hand, the passing away of the cold would improve conditions farther west and regions on the German Danube, the Main, Neckar, and the Rhine above and below the gorge as well as minor areas could increase the prosperity of their stock-raisers and perhaps encourage some cultivation. Herodotus and Apollonius allow the inference that Danubian Germany had Celtic-speaking peoples with a La Tène culture in the fifth century B.C. These warlike peoples conquering far and wide in the succeeding centuries, but lacking any large measure of organization, for a while hemmed the Germanic peoples in the colder north. But later on as prosperity spread northwards and Roman power made itself felt towards Rhine and Danube the Celtic-speaking groups were caught between two enemies. The northward spread of a measure of prosperity is attested in late La Tène times as far off as the lake region of Sweden, with extensions thence across the Baltic eastwards. A bronze neck-ring made by spiral winding of a metal strap and provided with a hook-fastening is a feature in the north; it also occurs in the British Isles.

The fading out of Celtic speech is understandable when this double pressure on south Germany is borne in mind and it is realized that writing was as yet unknown to any extent in this region, so language was more fluctuating than later on when, in Slavonic lands, an established ritual, and farther west the proximity of markets and the close organization of peasant communities attached people to their linguistic inheritance. The development of this attachment seems to be a feature that distinguishes historic from prehistoric phases in various regions of Europe. When the climate was recovering from its worst condition, settlement and improved plough-cultivation, apparently connected with the more general use of iron, became a feature in northern France, as will be stated again in the next chapter. We shall probably not be far wrong in suggesting that the parallel recovery in north Germany was accompanied by the development of the famous Germanic village-system, the Haufendorf or Gewanndorf of the German writers. The loess and related soils beneath both flanks of the Harz, and extensions to the west and north-west, seem to be a kernel-area for this type of settlement. It had, and often still has, houses heaped together without a trace of order, like the graves of the Urn-fields peasantry, and around them are the village lands in large fields each divided into many strips and each cultivated on a rotatory system.

Meitzen thought that the areas of erstwhile Celtic speech to the south and west of the Germanic area lacked this village scheme until they were conquered by Germans in Roman and post-Roman times. Since his time, however, traces of that scheme have been found in Westphalia and elsewhere in what had been areas of Celtic speech. None the less it is probable that differences did occur and it may be that schemes associated with stock-raisers in ancient Ireland, Wales, and elsewhere may be used to give clues to those utilized by the Celtic-speaking stock-raisers in central Europe in the wet period some centuries before Christ.

BOOKS

HUBERT, H. *The Rise of the Celts* (London, 1934).
HUBERT, H. *The Greatness and Decline of the Celts* (London, 1934).
EYRE, E. (Ed.). *European Civilization*, vol. ii (London, 1935).

II

The Iron Age in the West

THE use of bronze leaf-shaped swords and socketed axes characteristic of the Late Bronze Age lasted much longer in Britain than in the continental parts of western Europe.

In 1913 Déchelette summed up the current chronology of the Early Iron Age in France, defining two phases of Hallstatt culture, the first from 900 to 700 B.C., the second from 700 to 500 B.C. The latter was followed by the First La Tène phase, lasting from 500 to 300 B.C., this by the Second La Tène phase, from 300 to 100 B.C., and this again by the Third La Tène phase, stretching from 100 B.C. until Roman influence predominated. Following the lead of Jacobsthal, most students now believe that no trace of the style known as La Tène can anywhere be detected earlier than 450 B.C., while it did not become general, and certainly did not reach Britain, before 400 B.C. The distinctive features of the La Tène II phase, according to Viollier, do not make their appearance in Switzerland before 250 B.C., and this date has been accepted by Hawkes and Dunning for the Marne region; the appearance of this style in Britain is dated little if at all before 200 B.C. The La Tène III phase arose in north-east Gaul about 100 B.C., but reached the Thames estuary about 90 or 80 B.C., while another variety came to Southampton Water about 50 B.C. In most parts of Britain, including the

Sussex Downs, it had not arrived before the advent of the Roman legions.

The earliest iron swords found in France are copies of those of bronze, and the earliest Iron Age pottery, in both France and Britain, seems to be derived from continental models of the Late Bronze Age, especially of the Göritz type discussed in the last chapter.

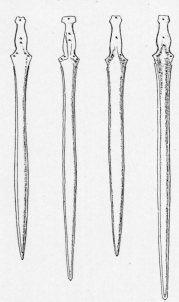

The urn-field culture persisted in France, especially near the north-east border and in the departments of Ain and Allier. Bronze swords, contemporary with objects of iron, have been found in the northern Jura and westward as far as the department of Cher; some have been discovered near Paris, also in the department of Lot and in other south-western regions. Long iron swords of early Hallstatt type have been found in Côte d'Or, Cher, and

FIG. 45. Hallstatt swords from France.

Cantal, indicating, as do the bronze swords, a movement, at least of culture, in the direction of the south-west during the transition from the Bronze to the Early Iron Age.

A number of iron daggers, belonging to the Second Hallstatt phase, with the pommels extending into a pair of *antennae*, have been found in the south-west; these indicate the extension of this phase of the culture as far as the Pyrenees. Iron ore was at that time discovered in various places in north-east France, and villages grew up around the mines; salt, too, valuable for preserving meat and also, perhaps, as a flux, was a factor determining settlements. In Saône et Loire this Early Iron Age culture took special root, and habitation sites are numerous, especially fortified camps, some of which, like the Camp de Chassey, had been occupied in neolithic times and may have retained their importance throughout the Bronze Age. It is interesting to note the utilization at this time of the departments of Côte d'Or, Saône et Loire, Lot, and several others that have limestone scarps, and would have been relatively dry during this cool and wet period.

It is doubtful whether we are justified in claiming a widespread true Hallstatt phase in the British Isles. Finger-tip potbuckets, of Hallstatt type, have turned up in quantities, but almost always with definitely La Tène associations, and it seems probable that the only true Hallstatt settlements were on the coast, though there are indications that the culture may have spread inland in Wiltshire; none of these settlements can be dated earlier than 700 B.C.

A considerable number of bronze Hallstatt swords have been recovered from the Thames between Reading and its mouth; this may imply some settlement by the banks of the river, but little evidence has turned up in support of this except a small urn, found in a gravel-pit on Southern Hill, Reading. It seems more likely that these objects came as the result of temporary visits, and the same may be true of the iron socketed axe-heads from Walthamstow and the iron spear-head found in a Bronze Age urn at Colchester. The discovery of a number of fragments of undoubted Hallstatt pottery near Eastbourne makes it clear that some settlement was effected upon the Sussex Downs, and it is believed that a few of the earthworks in that region, such as the Trundle, may have been used in this phase.

At Hengistbury Head there is also some evidence of a settlement in Hallstatt times, and the fortress at this place may perhaps be assigned to this date, though it was occupied well into the La Tène period; the pottery found here indicated relations with south-western France. The great settlement at All Cannings Cross, in the Vale of Pewsey, so well excavated by Mrs. Cunnington, has also been thought to go back to the Hallstatt

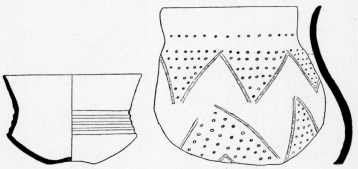

FIG. 46. Pottery from All Cannings Cross.

period. Here were found globular urns of the Deverel-Rimbury type, with raised mouldings impressed with finger-tip decoration; also a mass of well-formed pottery, made, however, without a turn-table or wheel. Implements of bone and antler were abundant, and the presence of loom-weights and spindle-whorls of chalk or baked clay shows that weaving was practised. The appearance, however, of two bronze *fibulae* of La Tène I type indicates that this settlement lasted on until the next period and raises the question whether the whole village may not be of La Tène date, though retaining earlier features in the pottery.

The south-westward trend in France of the Hallstatt culture mentioned above brought objects of this style to Provence, which, with north-western Italy, had belonged during the Bronze

Age to what is usually known as a Ligurian culture. Now that the climate was cooler and wetter than it had been, and the passes were less easily crossed, the links between the French and Italian sides became weaker. From southern France the Hallstatt culture penetrated Catalonia along the coast, bringing with it the characteristic biconical urns known from the Villanovan and other cultures, though the interior of that province long maintained its older tradition, in spite of a few intrusive ideas. The earliest Catalan finds show us a culture that lacks the iron sword, and this has led some to suggest that it dates from not long after 900 B.C. Those who recall the taboo on iron, so often mentioned in tradition, will wonder whether religious and even utilitarian reasons may not have caused men to refrain from placing iron swords in the graves of their departed, just as in earlier times there seems to have been objection to placing metal in graves when stone was giving way to copper and bronze. How slow was the penetration of iron weapons into the interior of Spain can be realized from the fact that moulds for casting socketed bronze axes and spear-heads have been found in a settlement in Aragon that on other grounds can be relegated to the fifth, perhaps even to the third, century B.C. In coastal Catalonia the graves of the earliest Iron Age usually contain little but brownish pottery, often polished and generally with incised ornament like that on contemporary urns from southern France, in a few of which iron neck-rings have been found. On Catalan sites a bronze chain, a bronze needle, and two bronze finger-rings have occurred, while in a somewhat later grave at Plâ de Gibrella has been found a dagger with horseshoe-shaped pommel, characteristic of the last Hallstatt phase in lands farther north, dating from about 500 B.C. About this time Catalonia was enjoying greater prosperity than was southern France, and tumuli containing urns and iron rings are found as far south as Almeria down the east coast of Spain

along which Greek colonies had been founded in the eighth
century B.C. The dagger with horseshoe-shaped pommel was
made nearly always in bronze, but sometimes in iron about the
sixth century B.C. in north-western Spain into which it probably spread from France rather
than via Catalonia. Atlantic Spain,
however, and Portugal were still
mainly in the grip of an older
tradition, from which they were
soon to be awakened by the general
stirring of craftsmanship, intercourse, and thought that followed
a redevelopment of maritime communications and the increase of
contacts with the classical world via
Tartessos in southern Spain as well
as through the Carcassonne Gap
in southern France.

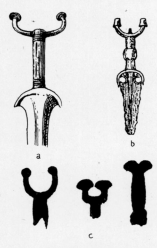

FIG. 47. Daggers with horseshoe-
shaped pommels. a, from Hallstatt; b, from Galicia in N.W.
Spain; c, development of pommel
in N.W. Spain.

In the last chapter we referred
to the rise of the La Tène culture
in the area that is now south Germany and its borders. The La Tène
fashions spread in France and seem
to have accompanied a considerable
increase in the population and an
improvement in agriculture, probably associated with a more
general use of a heavy wheeled plough in the fourth century B.C.,
as well as an infiltration of ideas from Greece, brought in through
Massilia or up the Austrian and Bavarian Danube basin, though
the Danube in Upper Austria was not a good line of communication.

The style of arms and art changed considerably and in many
parts the practice of burial, already important in the Hallstatt

phase in central Europe, rapidly superseded the Late Bronze Age habit of cremation, though not at first completely or universally. The change in funeral rites may well have been the result of propaganda rather than of a replacement of population, since we have nothing to contradict and much to support the suggestion that the La Tène culture spread from south Germany, where cremation had certainly been the rule in the late Bronze Age. Burials were still made in tumuli and, indeed, even in megalithic monuments in the west, and cremation also occurred, but in parts of France such as the Marne basin and Aquitaine the older forms of burial were superseded by flat graves arranged in cemeteries, with the bodies extended from east to west, the head being in the west; this practice was probably linked up with religious views concerning a future life, which may have accounted for the abandonment of cremation. The departments of Marne and Aisne and the country around Basel and Zürich as well as around Berne received considerable accessions of population; these districts seem to have contained few inhabitants during the earlier half of the Iron Age. In the case of Switzerland this relative emptiness may have been due to the cold and wet climatic phase about 900 to 700 B.C. or later; in the case of the French areas neither the dry soil of Marne nor the rich but heavy soils of Aisne had attracted to any extent the stock-raisers of the Hallstatt phase.

Though chieftains were buried in warrior garb the early La Tène age was not, apparently, much given to strife, since in many parts of Marne and Aisne the settlements were undefended; it was not until later that the well-fortified camps were redeveloped. The expansion of the population reached far beyond the bounds of France, for movements known as Celtic invasions affected Italy and troubled Rome in the fourth century B.C.; in the following century they spread to south-east Europe, and the Galatians went as far as Asia Minor.

The La Tène civilization did not immediately reach Atlantic Europe, but objects from that civilization and from the rising cultures of the Mediterranean trickled into the lands that had so long depended upon coastwise maritime communications.

During this period we find in the Iberian peninsula, especially near the north coast and in Galicia and Portugal, a mode of life that it has been customary to call the Castro culture from the fortified enclosures on hill-brows, built in many cases of dry stone walling or with steep scarps as defences. The Castros are found in groups, sometimes several obviously linked camps within an area of a few square miles. They usually show larger areas of presumably arable land between outer and inner ramparts than do the Iron Age earthworks of Britain. In mid-Portugal, where it extends southwards to beyond the Tagus, this Castro culture is influenced from Tartessos and the Mediterranean civilizations, by this time well established both in south-eastern Spain and in southern France. This is shown by the occurrence of wheel-made pottery and the development of rectangular stone buildings as well as by the objects found in the settlements. In the north, particularly in Galicia, some of the pottery is still hand-made, the huts are round and built of dry stone, while objects from Tartessos and the south-east of Spain, the area known as that of the Iberian culture, are relatively rare. In the north-west of the peninsula, which was cut off by the Iberian civilization from the original centres of La Tène culture, we can indeed say that there is no justification for speaking of a La Tène period. We are rather in the presence of something like what is known in Britain as the Iron Age B culture. This is a scheme of life having behind it the persistent megalithic tradition, that had by this time developed or more probably received the idea of the hill-brow and cliff fortress, eminently appropriate to seafarers, and that received La Tène features now and again. There are *fibulae* of early and middle

La Tène types, as well as swords with horseshoe-shaped handle-ends and neck-rings in bronze and in gold. While some think

Fig. 48. A castro in Galicia and its entrance enlarged.

that this Iron Age B culture began soon after 500 B.C., it is now more generally believed that its earliest spread must be relegated to the third century. In Le Morbihan Le Rouzic has examined Le Lizo, which has ramparts enclosing a megalithic tomb within a tumulus, as well as traces of later tombs, ovens, and hut foundations, dating from various periods, including that in which Roman influence was paramount. He has also drawn attention to numerous burials in Brittany dating from some time in the Iron Age after 500 B.C. These are under tumuli, often of heaped stones, an inheritance from older cultures, and at this period rectangular graves were made, often lined with stone and provided with corbelled roofs, even with tumuli heaped over them. Bracelets in bronze and in iron as well as glass beads have been found, but only a few *fibulae*.

In Brittany, too, Le Rouzic has found underground passages and chambers. He has also discovered in the Quiberon peninsula flat tombs with the bodies extended, obviously a fashion of the La Tène period, but this is exceptional, and again, as in the case of north-west Spain, we are dealing with a phase rather more like that of the Iron Age B culture in Britain. Comparative study is much needed, especially with regard to fortifications and graves, in order to clear up the arguments relating to the persistence or redevelopment of coastwise intercourse along the Atlantic shores in this period, after its decline, as far as Spain and Portugal were concerned, during the Middle Bronze Age.

In Britain we find two sequences of Early Iron Age cultures which Hawkes has called A and B. The A culture may be held to have begun with the settlement of Hengistbury, near Christchurch, Hants, the resettlement of the late Neolithic site of the Trundle on the Sussex Downs, and others comparable with these, but it is especially concerned with the people who crossed the English Channel at a rather later date, about 400 B.C. They derived their ideas from the district of the Marne and Aisne Rivers in north-eastern France, and spread especially across the narrow seas between Normandy and the Poole–Weymouth coast, though they also appeared on the Sussex shore and in the Thames estuary, using probably the ways across the straits of Dover. They knew how to make early La Tène pottery, and they also brought *fibulae* to Britain; the distribu-

tion of these *fibulae* or brooches is the best indication of the
domain of these people and it shows that they spread north-
eastwards along the Icknield Way. They also reached the
Cotswold country where later on their culture was displaced by

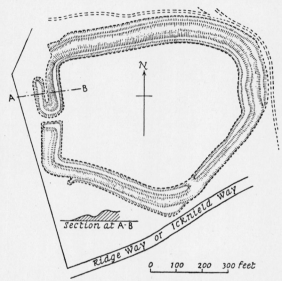

N

A ——— B

Section at A-B

Ridge Way or Icknield Way

0   100   200   300 feet

Fig. 49. Uffington hill-top camp on the Berkshire Downs.

that of the B people spreading from the south-west. There is
no doubt that they mingled with previous inhabitants and the
older rough ware decorated with finger-tip impressions continued to be made. The earlier stages of this culture are frequently characterized by small red-surfaced bowls.

Though some of their settlements were on the high ground,
lower-lying sites are not unknown, such as that by the side of
the alluvium at Theale in the Kennet valley; the most famous
of all, that at All Cannings Cross, which, as we have seen, may

have been founded in Hallstatt times, lies in the Vale of Pewsey at the foot of Tan Hill. They erected hill-top camps, usually on the crests of the Downs or on their spurs, and these appear to have been always devoid of retaining walls of stone; they often lack water-supplies; they are less frequently aggregated into groups than are those of the B people. Sometimes these culture camps occupy sites on which Causeway Camps of late neolithic days were built. On the Downs, also, Crawford has found traces of many small rectangular field-enclosures which are to be related to Iron Age occupation.

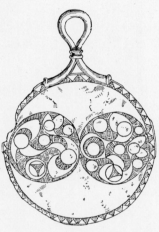

FIG. 50. 'Late Celtic' ornament.

Shortly before 200 B.C. the B culture entered Britain, via Cornwall and Devon. Parts of south Brittany and north-west Spain were occupied by related peoples who, like similarly distributed folk of the early metal age, were probably interested in metal. The A people were peasants, cultivating small rectangular plots with either a hoe or the simple Mediterranean plough or *araire*, but the B people were essentially traders. They had adopted, for pots and metal, curvilinear decoration originating at the head of the Adriatic and developed in central Europe into the Late Celtic style. This style contrasts with the simpler style of ornamentation used by the A people, though, on Boxford Common in Berkshire, there was found a cooking-pot decorated by the A people with a badly drawn wave-pattern copied from a vessel of the B people. Decorated pottery is, however, found on only a few sites and only in small quantities on some of these. B pots often have the handle pinched up by hand. There are many indications of local A and B features. Radford thinks that a third-century invasion accounts for the La Tène features at such places as All Cannings Cross, which, he would agree, was founded much earlier.

Earth-houses are known in western France, Cornwall, where they are called *fogou*, Ireland, and parts of Scotland, and, whatever their heritages from older cultures, they may be linked with Iron Age B. The people of this culture in Cornwall had relations along the Atlantic seaboard, for *fibulae*, resembling some from the Pyrenees, have been found in the settlement at Harlyn Bay, while at Chysauster Leeds found pottery that seems to have come from the Mediterranean; at Carn Brea were found a Numidian coin dating from before 100 B.C. and a number of gold coins from pre-Roman Gaul as well as one of the last century B.C. from Cyprus. In connexion with these movements there arises the interesting name of the Veneti. It is connected primarily with the head of the Adriatic, but also undoubtedly with south Brittany, as classical authors indicate and as the town of Vannes clearly shows. The name of the Wends, primarily south and south-east of the Baltic, appears to be associated in some way. It seems likely that the name Veneti became attached in the last two centuries B.C. to traders working mainly outside the area of the Greeks and Phoenicians, just as these two names had come to be used for traders in the one case of the Aegean ports of the Iron Age, and in the other case of Tyrian, Sidonian, and also earlier traders of the eastern Mediterranean. Associations of traders have been a marked feature of the world's life down to quite recent centuries as the names of the Hanseatic League, the Malays, and others show. In each case there is a special link with a cultural unit, that of Tyre and Sidon for the Phoenicians, and that of the Iron Age Aegean for the Greeks, and so on.

In the case of the Veneti it seems probable that an Illyrian element spreading from the eastern Alps of Austria to Italy and the north of what is now Yugoslavia, and allied to, if not included within, the peoples who spread the Hallstatt culture, also penetrated along the amber trade route to the south-east Baltic, and probably used the Rhine gorge-sides to get to the Low Countries, the home of the Belgae as Strabo tells us. The Belgae would be one of the results of the infusion of Hallstatt and possibly La Tène fashions into the life of the lower Rhine, which previously showed heritages from the tumulus and urnfields cultures.

But the traders also came into contact with the activities of the Atlantic route lingering on from the megalithic culture which we treated especially in *The Way of the Sea* and *Merchant Venturers in Bronze*. Indeed in many ways they are, as it were, a second edition of the peoples who spread over and around Europe a network of activities that is traceable through the study of beakers and megaliths described in those volumes. They show the Iron Age cultures modified by contact with the dry-walling skill attached to the megalithic tradition then still surviving along the Atlantic coasts.

Early Iron Age pile-dwellings in the swamp lands of the head of the Adriatic and in the Low Countries may be genetically connected with one another, but, even if they are not, the latter are almost certainly related to those of the B culture in the Glastonbury Marshes, which were then a tidal bay like Poole harbour. The pile-dwellings were built on mud-banks near the Isle of Avalon and at Meare, sites much like those of the Frisian coast. Thence the B people moved north-eastwards along the Oolite ridge displacing the culture of the A people from the Cotswolds.

On these hills they rebuilt the hill-forts erected earlier by the A people, using a revetment of dry stone walling, but they do not seem to have crossed the Upper Thames. They extended,

Fig. 51a. Glastonbury Pile Village.

however, in the direction of Cleveland, and were probably responsible for the lake dwellings of Yorkshire. In Yorkshire the B culture was affected by a movement along the North Sea coasts from France avoiding the territory of the A people, and this movement brought with it the custom of chariot burials like those known from Lake Maggiore, Bern, south Germany, and eastern France. The B people of Britain possibly also

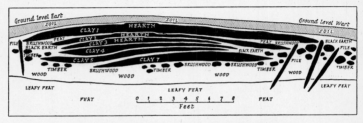

FIG. 51*b*. Section of Glastonbury Pile Village.

received reinforcements near the Wash, responsible for settlements on the north Norfolk coast.

Varley has revealed at Maiden Castle, Bickerton, Cheshire, a rampart with a core of layers of sand and of poles laid lengthways, crossways, and diagonally, the core being covered by pebbles tightly wedged and the whole resembling what Caesar calls a *murus gallicus*. Analogous work is known from Corley, Warwickshire, and from the north side of the Ochil hills. Maiden Castle, Dorset, was occupied like many another earthwork well into Roman times and contains foundations of a Roman building.

The areas of Iron Age cultures are rather like those of kingdoms of legendary history: Cornwall, the south-west, the basis of the B people; Loegria, the south-east, the region of the A people, Albany, north of Nene or Trent, into which the B culture spread. Dunwallo, king of the B people, triumphs over

other kings and makes safe roads which Belinus improves. Roads
do become more definite in the La Tène period. Belinus has
connexions with the Senones, admirably illustrated by the
distribution of early La Tène *fibulae*.

Late Bronze Age peoples reached the western isles of Scotland, possibly from Ireland, while Iron Age A pottery occurs

FIG. 52. The Broch of Mousa, Shetland.

in Aberdeenshire, Morayshire, and Shetland. To the east coast
came later, from the European plain, people who made ramparts and then vitrified their surfaces. They had La Tène
fibulae but are a group distinct from all others of the British
Iron Age. They spread to the west, the Clyde, Galloway, and
Ireland. The crannogs, or lake-dwellings, are analogous with
those of Iron Age Yorkshire and, like them, represent an
expression of Iron Age B culture.

On the west side of Scotland the distribution of Iron Age
remains shows the same analogy with that of the megalithic cult,
which began so long before but continued down to historic

times. In west Scotland and the Isles are found smallish structures of stone forming ramparts and strongholds, and, whatever their period may be, the famous brochs have a closely related distribution. In some caves and elsewhere in south-west Scotland there have been found objects recalling those known from Glastonbury. It is thus probable that there was a good deal of infiltration of ideas up and down the west coast of Britain. The fine work of Curle at Jarlshof, Shetland, has just revealed a settlement with transitions from bronze to iron, as well as earth-houses.

J. W. Jackson has just discovered in Antrim pottery related in general to that of Iron Age A and, also in pottery, a female figure with a head-dress, provisionally considered to be a representation of the Mother Goddess.

The abundance of fortifications of presumed Iron Age date in Ireland, including the Raths, is a marked feature.

In the last century B.C. peoples known under the name of Belgae, and equipped with a Late La Tène civilization, spread across the straits of Dover, while another group of them a generation later came to Southampton Water.

A short statement must be added concerning the vexed question of language. Since the Greeks and Romans appear to have met in most parts of Europe peoples speaking various tongues that belonged to the Aryan group, those languages must have been in existence for some centuries prior to the beginning of our era, and the Italic, Celtic, Teutonic, and other forms had already taken shape in various regions. This justifies the belief that the Iron Age populations of Europe used, for the most part at least, some form of Aryan speech; we may also suppose that in south Germany, Austria, and France some Celtic dialects were in use, while near the south and west of the Baltic the speech was Teutonic. How far back in time the Celtic dialects go in most of Germany it is not yet possible to

say, but it is interesting, at any rate, to speculate on the origin
of Aryan speech on or near the south Russian steppe, and its
dispersal over Europe by means of one of the movements of
people who spread thence far and wide before the Iron Age.
The least remote of these movements was that which brought
the horse into Europe and developed the sword, of bronze at
first, as a prominent weapon. We know, too, that contemporary
and probably associated with this movement came improvements
in agriculture, including better forms of wheat; this permitted
a growth in the population and allowed of a more definite
organization of the peasantry during the Middle Bronze Age.

If the forms of Aryan speech spread at this time, they would
doubtless have undergone various sound-changes, following
contacts with people of diverse physical characters. A long
upper lip helps its possessor to say *p* or *b* where a somewhat
shorter-lipped person is inclined to say *f* or *v*, or a really short-
lipped individual may use a sound approximating to *k* or *q*.
The shape and size of the tongue, the character of the bite, the
resonance of the palate, lower in some types than in others, all
help to produce modification of sounds and of intonation. It is
very probable that sound-changes also developed of themselves
with lapse of time, as Grimm's Law has suggested.

Following this line of thought it will be seen that there might
well be difficulty in determining when a language, in the course
of evolution, first became Celtic, Teutonic, or Italic. However
that may be, there is little doubt that the movement of people
which brought a Hallstatt culture from south Germany to
Catalonia, brought also some form of Celtic speech, for we find
there old Celtic place-names, and this language must have
become widespread in France during the Iron Age, even if it
had not been present there before. The Celtic dialects must
have reached north-west Spain too, at the latest with the rise
of the Castro culture. It is highly probable that the Iron Age B

culture affected the languages of Cornwall, Wales, Ireland, and Scotland, though it is difficult to imagine that the speech of the people who brought with them leaf-shaped swords to Britain and Ireland was anything but some form of Celtic. At any rate the influence of Iron Age B culture played upon west Britain and Ireland, while that of culture A was at work in south-east England. The backgrounds of tradition were different in the two cases, and in the south-west of Britain there was inevitable pressure from the south-east before and during Roman times.

We know that the language spoken in England immediately before the arrival of the Romans was a variety of Celtic speech, associated later with Welsh, Cornish, and Breton; linguists give it the name of Brythonic. The languages known as Erse, Manx, and Gaelic, on the other hand, are called Goidelic. Some writers have held that we must assume the occurrence of two waves coming in succession, the earlier carrying Goidelic and the later Brythonic dialects, and that the latter drove the former towards the west.

An alternative speculation, that is less hampered by the apparent absence of real Goidelic place-names in England and most of Wales, is that a Celtic dialect spread with the leaf-shaped swords and underwent divers modifications in different parts, becoming Brythonic under the influence of contacts between the Iron Age A people and the people that they found there, and spreading later to the west of Britain, where the Iron Age B people were also bringing modifications which, in the isolated areas of Ireland, Man, and west Scotland, gave rise to the Goidelic dialects. The Brythonic languages emphasize *b* and *p* where the Goidelic use *k* and *q*, and so the two groups are sometimes called P-Celts and Q-Celts. That Q-Celtic was spoken in south Britain before an invasion from Ireland in fairly late Roman times has been strongly denied. There is probably no profitable argument here, but we suspect that west Britain was

going the way of the Q-groups when pressure from the more or
less Brythonic-speaking peoples set in during Roman times.

BOOKS

Fox, Sir C. *Personality of Britain* (Cardiff, Nat. Mus., 1933).
Kendrick, T. D., and Hawkes, C. F. C. *Archaeology in England and Wales,*
1914–1931 (London, 1932).
Cunnington, M. E. *All Cannings Cross* (Devizes, 1923).
Childe, V. G. *Prehistory of Scotland* (London, 1935).
Eyre, E. (Ed.) *European Civilization,* vol. ii (London, 1935).
Leeds, E. T., *Celtic Ornament* (Oxford, 1933).
British Museum Guide to the Antiquities of the Early Iron Age (London, 1925).
County Archaeologies, especially Hencken, H. O., *Cornwall* (London, 1933).
Dobson, D. P., *Somerset* (London, 1931), and Elgee, F., *Yorkshire* (London,
1933).

12

Philosophers and Barbarians

IN the volumes of the *Corridors of Time* an attempt has been
made to pick out the outstanding feature of each phase of the
evolution of civilization, perhaps sometimes with rather too
close an eye on our own part of the world, as in *The Way of the
Sea* and *Merchant Venturers in Bronze.* In the volume next to
these two, however, the main theme was the very wide one of
the advent of *The Horse and the Sword.* Wherever and when-
ever man first developed his partnership with the horse in war
and pageantry, that domestic animal at any rate became far
more widespread in the second millennium B.C. and gave its
riders wider opportunities of movement and of power over those
who were not on horseback. The hero-swordsman on his horse
could seek adventure and sometimes found fortune, and there
are thence records of dynasties in China leading on to the Chou
(*c.* 1100 B.C.), of the Indo-Aryans dominating north India from
about 1500 B.C., of the power of Mitanni in south-west Asia

with predecessors and successors until we get to the Medes and Persians and, though we lack records for Europe, archaeology suggests the spread of horse and sword, and folk-lore and mythology add to this such stories as those of Odin.

Bronze became widespread and brought a considerable development of craftsmanship. Better breeds of wheat spread, at least in Europe, when peasantries became more numerous as well as better equipped. Exchange became a more marked feature and cities had already long been in existence in various parts of a belt stretching from Greece to China. It is obvious that there was in many places, for at least some of the people, the leaders in other words, the possibility of a considerable surplus over and above immediate needs. While the steppe of inner Asia and south Russia remained dry and hot, there was apparently much movement and disturbance that led its horsemen to dominate cultivators in the wetter lands. And in this way the cavalry-prince was sometimes metamorphosed into a settled administrator with luxury in his court and with subjects of alien tradition often needing to be humoured, especially if they were his wives. There was thus the serious need to rise above the traditionalist attitude and the old method of living within a tradition that remained unquestioned. There must now be an attempt to combine traditions, to synthesize, to look at any rate some distance towards the universal. What wonder then that in China, India, Iran, Israel, and Greece we find a development of ethical teaching and a criticism of ritualistic tradition? It is not that new and abstract thought passed in some mysterious way from land to land, though this type of transfer must have done a great deal for Israel at least. Rather is it that analogous, almost homologous, circumstances in many lands that already had millennia of civilization behind them led to similar, and yet in detail diverse, manifestations of thought about man's place in the universe and his conduct of life in the various societies that had been growing even ever so little beyond the phase of rule of custom, invested with a holy dignity by being wrapped in a mythological robe, the cut of which was as yet exempt from question.

The new order cries out against observances and ritual and asks for righteousness, a sense of right-doing which is increasingly understood to transcend social barriers and to apply between men of diverse ranks and peoples. The teachers of the new order may more or less utilize cosmological fancies or eschatological notions current in their day as a means of promoting the understanding of their ethical notions by the unlearned, but their interest is in right conduct, and, because of this in particular, the diverse expressions of this interest in various lands differ characteristically from one another.

China had an old-established peasantry engaged especially in lowland and terrace cultivation, often with irrigation and a general scheme that maintained the fertility of the soil by deposits of alluvial mud from floods or irrigation water. Moreover, the special emphasis on cultivation and the relatively small amount of stock-raising had led to the careful utilization of plant-waste and refuse generally as manure, while the family system with its veneration of the graves of the ancestors had led to large families and small holdings, and skill had been devoted to such processes as bedding out and sometimes selection of plants and seeds. Thus society was focused to a large extent upon the ideal of maintenance down the generations and skill found scope in care of the soil; and the control of larger areas had become a mark of social rank and an indication of a good family tradition. Save towards the frontiers there was relatively little conflict between crop-growers and stock farmers with their diverse ideas and outlooks, and groups from across the frontiers who conquered and founded dynasties were absorbed one after another into the Chinese system. Under these circumstances the rise of thought was along lines of a social ethic with the maintenance of the family as its chief feature.

Reference has already been made to Lao Tzu and Confucius as the two best-known names among Chinese sages. Here we are concerned with some relations of their teaching to the life and tradition of China as summarized above. Neither seems to have laid claim to a divine revelation or to have emphasized the idea of a personal deity. Confucius characteristically held that society was an ordinance of heaven based on five great relationships, that of friendship aiming at the cultivation of virtue, and four others, namely those of ruler and subject, husband and wife, father and son, elder and younger brother in which it became the one to rule with benevolence and the other to follow with sincerity, with the guiding principle in both cases of doing unto others as you would they should do unto you. Lao Tzu, a mystic, was apparently imbued with the idea of simplicity, of becoming as a little child, of casting away set ambitions of precedence, of knowing and following Tao. Both appear to have relied on conscience, that is on a guiding principle from within, and to have accepted the traditional ritual of their people, but, so far as one can estimate from very scant information, their conservative tendencies did not make them opponents of freedom of thought.

In India the setting of the scene was different. Conquerors had reached India centuries before there appeared the sages who have remained in memory. They were an aristocracy over a peasantry practising rites of immemorial antiquity and cultivating and keeping cattle with, apparently, a tradition embodying far less skill than was current in China. The caste system gave men and women their position in life, and social grading was a far more important feature than in China, whatever may have been the state of affairs in earlier times in the latter country. The clash of territorial and other political ambitions of aristocratic groups was combined with a sense of their being a cultured minority facing innumerable hordes of the common people between whom and themselves was a great gulf fixed. Yet those hordes were so numerous that it behoved the aristocracy to be careful at times not to stir up their prejudices.

Under these circumstances the aristocratic thinkers must be concerned less with what they would feel to be the impossible task of changing the life of the common people than with the desire to seek a way of peace and sanctity above the turmoil of ambitious rivalries and consequent wars and devastations. The original gods of the conquerors, as we have said, fell into the background as their meaning in the actual life of the now settled rulers diminished. The ritual of the common people, on the other hand, largely through its influence in maintaining the cycle of agricultural activities and social life, tended to become the basis of a general religion which, however, was not likely to satisfy leisured thinkers. We have noticed briefly some efforts to expound ethical principles, but the most characteristic feature of Indian thought was expressed by the Buddha in his emphasis on Nirvana as a goal upon attaining which men would be liberated from all bodily forms and activities. His ideas, like those of the Chinese, did not emphasize a personal God, but differed from those of China's sages in giving less attention to society and in elaborating a vision of the contemplative life that hindered nothing on its upward way through countless transmigrations of the soul towards its ultimate goal of absorption in the universal.

The teaching of Zoroaster came to be a feature of Persian life and thought, and here again circumstances were very different. Cavalrymen, gathered around a leader and trained to ride, to draw the bow, and to speak the truth, came to be a people under a king who was not faced with the uncountable masses of the Indian peasantry, nor had they the opportunity to develop the intensive cultivation of the soil and its attachment to the family that characterized China. The horse and the loyalty that goes with it were the basis of their ideals and were made to stand out in contrast with disloyalty and evil. Loyalty to the person of the ruler helped no doubt to attach the notion of personality to the ideal and we have the supreme God, Ahura-Mazda, striving to maintain mastery over the forces of evil personified as Ahriman.

Dualism rather than Monism, Personality rather than Society, knightly virtue (if we may borrow a later term) rather than middle-class neighbourliness or aristocratic contemplation, were the features of Iranian thought. But, as has already been stated in Chapter 6, these knightly ideas were developed with a measure of toleration. Ahura-Mazda was the supreme expression of Divinity, but Jahweh, Amen-Ra, and many others could figure as the gods of conquered peoples, and the development of thought brought the vital idea that all were in the last resort expressions of the belief in the spiritual power wherein all live and move and have their being. Rulers from the steppe, the Iranians, like those who penetrated into China and those who conquered India, had the faculty of absorbing ideas from the people they met, of modifying their tradition to meet new circumstances, and to this they added an ethic that tried to rise above despotic exploitation towards a universal synthesis apparently transcending the thoughts of the Chinese sages and furnishing a stronger social motive power than the Indian sages were able to infuse into the people of that land of contrasts. It is interesting and most important to realize that these three, broadly contemporary, movements of thought with marked resemblances, if also with characteristic diversities, do not seem to lend themselves to interpretation along lines of a transmission of culture from one to another. They are to a large extent separate and independent movements, however much all three may owe to the background of the conquests of horsemen of the steppe followed by adaptations to very diverse circumstances in China, India, and Iran.

The expression of the same tendencies of thought in Israel can be followed in the prophetic books of the Old Testament Scriptures and in the New Testament. The power of evil is crystallized out as Satan and the ethical parallels with the other schemes of thought mentioned here are too obvious to need emphasis. Jahweh becomes the concept of the Universal Deity, but the movement of return of exiles gives a glow of emotion to many a reference to Zion. It is sometimes the consecrated centre of national aspirations of a people deeply steeped in conscious apartness during their sojourn by the waters of Babylon, and sometimes it becomes the ideal city of mankind, the spiritual focus that is to draw all men to its gates.

In Egypt the insurgence of thought came early, too early perhaps to have its full influence. At any rate the heresies introduced under Ikhnaton were suppressed, so far as we can judge, by a priestly revival which fixed its rule upon Egypt for centuries and appears to have made it weak, effete in fact, so that it collapsed before the rising power of Persia.

Whereas the Chinese agricultural system contrived to maintain the organization of society with the family emphasized as the most important unit around which almost everything was gathered, in the Greek lands with their specialization of crafts and their trade there was a tendency to make neighbourhood take the place of kinship to some extent in social organization. Thence there grew systems of law regulating intercourse between unrelated people while agreements, contracts, coinage, and so on came to add complexity to commercial and political relations but at the same time to spread the field of supply and demand and to raise standards of living for the more fortunate as well, no doubt, as to develop new possibilities of exploitation of the more helpless. The loosening of the domination of the kinship group and the leisure the more fortunate acquired naturally led to reflective thought as well as to political efforts.

Speculation on the origin of all things, on life and mind, on ideas of the gods, theories of the ideal state and the relations of its members to it, stories of olden time and of other people's ways all spread, while aesthetics claimed special interest and attention. The emphasis on the individual, within the limits of this life, his idealization in art, his powers of creating and enjoying beauty in the society of his fellows, may be set over against the major emphasis on a social ethic in China, and on the fate of man beyond the limits of this life in Buddhist India.

Around the belt of civilization discussed in this chapter lay a broad fringe of barbarous peoples without writing, but often apparently well above the 'savage' level. Among them penetrate ideas from the belt of civilization, as witness Mediterranean, basically Greek, ideas in the designs used by Scythians and in those used by Celtic-speaking peoples in the west (for example, in the La Tène phase). Of the spread beyond India south-eastwards it must suffice to say that apparently the main movement was delayed some centuries. The movement towards intertropical Africa faced the difficulty that this great region had had very little Bronze Age experience and had thus largely missed the training that peoples farther north had acquired in that phase. The knowledge of iron spread into torrid Africa, how soon we do not know, but this was accompanied by little enough of the later developments of civilization; an abstract social ethic and philosophical outlook could not be grafted directly on what was probably in essentials at least Stone Age life.

The examples, drawn from the major groups inhabiting a belt from China to Greece, the product of a long succession of generations that had gradually built up a settled social life, suffice to show that parallel stirrings of thought took characteristically diverse forms as they developed, but all involved some nearer approach to a general or abstract ethic than had previously been known. The change is that which in theological terms is described as the change from the old to the new dispensation; in archaeology it is essentially the gradation from prehistoric to historic times. Henceforth, abstract notions, especially in ethics and the underlying social motive power, begin their historic struggle for recognition. They are henceforth consciously realized in a far more complete way than heretofore, so they may be preached and may claim converts; the day of religious propaganda has dawned.

INDEX